Brilliant Parents, Fascinating Teachers

DR AUGUSTO CURY

Copyright © 2024 Dr Augusto Cury.

All rights reserved. This book or any portion thereof may not be reproduced or used in any manner whatsoever without the express written permission of the publisher except for the use of brief quotations in a book review.

This book was updated in 2024.

ISBN: 978-1-965965-00-9 (Paperback)

DEDICATION

I dedicate this book to a
very important person in my life:

_____

You sacrificed your dreams so I could dream.
You shed tears so I could be happy.
You endured sleepless nights so I could rest peacefully.
You believed in me, regardless of my mistakes.
Being an educator means being a poet of love.
Never forget that I will carry
a piece of your being within my own being forever.

_____/_____/_____

Table of Contents

Foreword 1
Where The Youth are Heading 3

Part 1: Seven habits of good parents… and of those who are brilliant parents 9
Good parents give gifts; Brilliant parents give their own being 11
Good parents nourish the body; Brilliant parents nurture the personality 17
Good parents correct mistakes; Brilliant parents teach how to think 22
Good parents prepare their children for success; Brilliant parents prepare them for failure 27
Good parents talk; Brilliant parents engage in conversation as friends 31
Good parents provide information; Brilliant parents tell stories 36
Good parents give opportunities; Brilliant parents never give up 39

Part 2: Seven Habits of Good Teachers… and of those who are Fascinating Teachers 43
Good teachers are eloquent; Fascinating teachers understand the working of the mind 45
Good teachers have methodology; Fascinating teachers have sensitivity 51
Good teachers educate logical intelligence; Fascinating teachers educate emotion .. 53
Good teachers use the memory as information storage; Fascinating teachers use it as a foundation for the art of thinking 55
Good teachers are temporary masters; Fascinating teachers are unforgettable ones. 59
Good teachers correct behavior; Fascinating teachers resolve conflicts in the classroom 61
Good teachers prepare students for a profession; Fascinating teachers prepare them for life 64

Part 3: The Educator's Seven Deadly Sins 67
Correcting in public 69
Expressing authority with aggressiveness 72

Being overly critical: obstructing a kid's childhood 75
Punishing when angry and setting limits without explanations........................... 77
Being impatient and giving up on educating... 80
Failing to keep their word 82
Destroying hope and dreams... 84

Part 4: The Five Roles of Human Memory 87
Memory: The Secret Box of Personality... 88
Memory registration is involuntary.. 89
Emotion determines the quality of recording 91
Memory cannot be deleted.. 93
The degree to which memory windows open depends on emotion 95
Pure recollection does not exist... 97

Part 5: The School of Our Dreams 99
The School of Life Project 101
Background music in the classroom... 102
Seating in a circle or U-shape 104
Inquired presentation: The art of doubting... 107
Dialogical presentation: the art of asking questions... 110
Being a storyteller 113
Humanizing knowledge 116
Humanizing the teacher: crossing their story 119
Educating the self-esteem: praising before criticizing.. 124
Managing thoughts and emotions 128
Engaging in social projects... 131

Part 6: The Great Tower Story 137
Who are the most important workers in society?... 138
Final Considerations 145
A Tribute to The Teachers 146
A Tribute to The Parents.. 147

Bibliographic References.. 148

Foreword

It is an immense personal and professional satisfaction to know that this book has already sold more than 3 million copies, having been published in dozens of countries, touching people from different cultures and intellectually challenging them with its message. I wrote "Shining Parents, Fascinating Teachers" not for heroes, but for those who understand that educating is practicing the most beautiful and complex art of existence.

Educating is having hope for the future, even if the present disappoints us. It is like sowing with wisdom and reaping with patience. It is like being a prospector who searches for the treasures of the heart. This is the goal of all educators who strive for excellence, of those who seek to understand the workings of the mind, who stimulate young people for the art of thinking, observing, and internalizing.

In this book, I present important tools that help shape thinkers and teach how to expand emotion, broaden the horizons of intelligence, and produce quality of life. It will speak to the hearts of parents and teachers who fight for the same dream: the development of mental health, happiness, and the most important functions of intelligence.

Parents and teachers who are full of rules and overly-logical are able to operate machines, but are not equipped to guide human beings. Parents and teachers who are experts in pointing out mistakes and criticizing errors may be qualified to manage companies, but not to develop thinkers.

We cannot control the shaping process of the personality of our youth. It requires maturity, flexibility, creativity, and the ability to surprise others. Basically, it requires working on the habits of the shining – or brilliant – parents and fascinating teachers to help our children and students develop healthy, inventive, bold, resilient, secure, altruistic, tolerant, patient, and generous minds.

Consider the challenges of cultivating the mental soil of children and teenagers so that they learn to think before reacting and to expose, instead of impose, their ideas. How can we stimulate this noble emotional phenomenon? Think about the difficulties of teaching young people to protect their emotions – how can we work on this noble function of intelligence when we, as adults, barely understand or think about it?

Consider the educational journey that parents and teachers must undertake in the psyche of teenagers so that they can learn how to manage thoughts, debate ideas, cope with losses, express their opinions, and respect those who think differently. Educating is a great challenge, perhaps the greatest of all. My intention is to guide you through this complex and fascinating journey.

Throughout my experience as a psychiatrist, writer and psychology researcher, I have helped many people change the course of their lives and see education from a different perspective. I hope to continue contributing to the shaping of thinkers, not only in the classroom but also at home and in businesses.

This book is dedicated to all the parents and teachers, psychologists, social workers, human resources practitioners, young people, and anyone who wishes to unveil some secrets of the personality, understand the workings of the mind, and enrich their relationships.

Where The Youth are Heading

There is a world to be discovered inside every child and every young person. Only those who are imprisoned within their own world cannot discover it.

Our generation wanted to give the best to our children and young people. We dreamed great dreams for them. We tried to give them the best toys, clothes, trips, and schools. We didn't want them to walk in the rain, get hurt on the streets, be injured by homemade toys, or face the hardships we went through. We put a television in the living room. Some parents, with more resources, put a television and a computer in each of their children's room. Others filled their children's schedules with activities, enrolling them in foreign languages, computer, and music courses.

They had excellent intentions, but they didn't know that children needed to have a childhood, that they needed to invent, take risks, experience frustration, have time to play, and be enchanted with life. They didn't realize how much creativity, happiness, boldness, and security in adults depend on the matrices of the child's memory and emotional energy. They didn't understand that electronic games, manufactured toys, the internet, and the excess of activities obstructed the childhood of their children.

We have created an artificial world for children, and we paid a high price. We generated serious consequences in the territory of emotion, in the "theater" of thoughts, and in the soil of their memory. Let's look at some of the consequences.

Obstructing the intelligence of kids and teens

We hoped that young people would be supportive, entrepreneurial, and that they would love the art of thinking in the 21st century. But many live alienated, lacking thoughts about the future, determination, or life projects. We thought that the problem of loneliness would be solved, since we learn languages in school and live crammed into elevators, workplaces, and clubs. However, people have not learned to talk about themselves, they are afraid to be exposed, they live confined in their own world. Parents and children live isolated, rarely crying together or discussing their dreams, sorrows, joys, or frustrations.

In school, the situation is worse. Teachers and students spend years together inside the classroom, but they are strangers to each other. They hide behind books, booklets, and computers. Is it the illustrious teachers' fault? No! As we will see, the fault lies in the sick educational system that has been dragging on for centuries.

Children and young people learn how to deal with logical facts but, they do not know how to deal with failures and mistakes. They learn how to solve Math problems but do not know how to solve their existential conflicts. They are trained to make calculations and get them right, but life is full of contradictions: emotional issues cannot be calculated, nor do they have an exact answer.

Are young people prepared to deal with disappointments? No, they are not! They are trained only for success. Living without problems is impossible. Suffering either builds us or destroys us. We should use suffering to build wisdom. Yet who cares about wisdom in the Information Age?

Our generation has produced information like no other before, but we do not know what to do with it all. We rarely use this information to improve our quality of life. Do you do things outside your schedule that give you pleasure? Do you try to manage your thoughts to have a more peaceful mind? We have become work machines and we are turning our children into learning machines.

Using the roles of memory for the wrong purpose

We turned our children's memory into a storage unit. Does memory have this purpose? Definitely not! We will see that memory has been used incorrectly by the school for centuries.

Is there any recollection? Numerous teachers and psychologists worldwide believe without a shadow of a doubt that there is recollection. That's wrong! There is no pure recollection of the past; the past is always reconstructed! We should be shaken by this statement: The past is always reconstructed with micro or macro differences in the present.

We will see that there are several misconceptions in science about the fantastic world of the mind working and the human memory. I am convinced of it, as a psychiatrist and author of one of the few current theories about the process of thinking construction, that we are obstructing the intelligence of children and their pleasure of living with the excess of information that we are offering them. Our memory has become a repository of useless information.

Most of the information we learn will not be organized in memory nor used in intellectual activities. Imagine a bricklayer who gathered stones throughout his life to build a house. After building it, he has no idea what to do with the piles of stones that are left over. He spent most of his time uselessly.

Knowledge has multiplied, and the number of schools has expanded like never before; however, we have not been producing thinkers. Most young people, including university students, accumulate piles of "stones" but build very few brilliant ideas. No wonder they have lost the joy of learning. School is no longer a pleasant adventure.

At the same time, the media has seduced them with quick and ready stimuli. They have become lovers of emotional fast food. Without any effort on their part, screens transport young people into an exciting sporting event, inside an aircraft, the heart of a battle, and a dramatic police conflict. This bombardment of stimuli is not harmless. It acts on an unconscious phenomenon in my area of research, which is called psycho-adaptation, increasing the threshold of pleasure in real life. Over time, children and adolescents lose pleasure in the small stimuli of daily life.

They need to do a lot of things to have a little pleasure, which generates fluctuating, unstable, and dissatisfied personalities. We have a complex leisure industry. We should have the happiest generation of young people who have ever walked this earth. But we have produced a generation of dissatisfied individuals.

We are informing, instead of forming

We are not educating emotions or stimulating the development of the most important functions of intelligence, such as contemplating beauty, thinking before reacting, exposing ideas instead of imposing them, managing thoughts, or having an entrepreneurial spirit. We are informing young people and not forming their personalities. Young people know more and more about the world they are in, although almost nothing about the world they are. At most, they know the living room of their own personality. Can you picture a worse loneliness than that? Human beings are strangers to themselves!

Education has become dry, cold, and lacking emotional spice. Young people rarely know how to apologize, recognize their limits, or put themselves in others' shoes. What is the outcome? Never has medical and psychiatric knowledge expanded so much, and never have people had so many emotional disorders and psychosomatic illnesses. Depression rarely affected children in the past. Today, many children are depressed and lack enthusiasm for life. Pre-teens and teenagers are developing obsessions, panic disorders, phobias, shyness, aggression, and other anxious disorders.

Millions of young people are taking drugs. They do not understand that drugs can skip stages of life and make them rapidly age emotionally. The momentary pleasures of drugs destroy the golden goose of emotion. I have met and treated countless young drug abusers, but none of them were happy.

And what about stress? Not only is it common to detect stressed adults, but also young people and children. They often have headaches, gastritis, muscle aches, excessive sweating, and constant fatigue that are affected by emotional backgrounds.

We must engrain this sentence and not forget it anymore: the lower the quality of education, the greater the role of psychiatry will be in this century. Will we passively watch the antidepressant and tranquilizer industry become one of the most powerful of the 21st century? Will we passively watch our children become victims of the social system we created? What should we do when dealing with this problem?

Searching for shining parents and fascinating teachers

We must seek solutions that directly address the problem. We need to know something about how the mind works and thus change some pillars of education. Theories no longer work. Good teachers are stressed and producing students who are unprepared for life. Good parents are confused and raise their children under conflicts. However, there is great hope, though there are no magical solutions.

Currently, being good is not enough, as the education crisis requires us to seek excellence. Parents need to acquire the habits of shining – or brilliant – parents to revolutionize education. Teachers need to incorporate the habits of fascinating educators to efficiently operate in the small, although infinite world of their students' personalities. Each habit practiced by educators can contribute to developing fundamental characteristics of young people's personalities. There are more than fifty of these characteristics. However, it is difficult to find a young person who has five of them well developed.

We need to be educators well above average if we want to shape intelligent and happy human beings, capable of surviving in this stressful society. The good news is that parents, regardless of whether they are rich or poor, and teachers who work in rich or needy schools can equally practice the habits and techniques that I propose here.

An excellent educator is not a perfect human being, but someone who has the serenity to empty themselves and the sensitivity to always learn something.

PART 1

Seven habits of good parents...
and of those who are brilliant parents

Children do not need colossal parents, but human beings who speak their language and can penetrate their hearts.

1

Good parents give gifts;
Brilliant parents give their own being

> *This habit of brilliant parents contributes to developing in their children: self-esteem, emotional protection, coping skills for setbacks and disappointments, the capacity to filter unpleasant stimuli, to dialogue, and to listen.*

Good parents meet, within their means, the desires of their children. They organize birthday parties, purchase sneakers, clothes, electronics, and plan trips for them. Brilliant parents give something incomparably more valuable to their children – something all the money in the world cannot buy: their being, their story, their experiences, their tears, their time. Brilliant parents, when it is possible, give material gifts to their children, but they do not encourage them to be consumers because they understand that consumerism can crush emotional stability, raise tension, and provide only superficial pleasures. Parents who live to give gifts to their children are remembered for a moment. Parents who care about giving their story to their children become unforgettable.

Do you want to be a brilliant father or mother? Have the courage to talk about the saddest days of your life with your children. Dare to talk about your hardships of the past. Share your adventures, dreams, and the happiest moments of your existence. Humanize yourself. Turn your relationship with your children into an adventure. Be aware that educating is to penetrate into each other's world. Many parents work to give the world to their children but they forget to open the book of their life to them. Unfortunately, their children will only admire them on the day they die.

Why is it critical for the development of children's personalities that parents make themselves known? Because this is the only way to educate emotion and create solid and deep bonds. The more inferior the life of an animal, the less dependent it is on its parents. As mammals, children rely heavily on their parents for survival, not only through instinct but also through learning from their parents' experiences.

In our species, this dependence is intense. Why? Because learned experiences are more important than instinctive ones. A seven-year-old child is very immature and dependent on their parents, while many animals of the same age are already elderly. How does this learning happen? I could write hundreds of pages on this subject, but in this book, I will only comment on some phenomena involved in the process.

Learning depends on the daily recording of thousands of external (visual, auditory, tactile) and internal (thoughts and emotional reactions) stimuli in the memory matrices. Annually, we archive millions of experiences. Unlike computers, the recording in our memory is involuntary, produced by the AMR (Automatic Memory Recording) phenomenon.

In computers, we decide what to save, but in human memory, saving does not depend on our will. All the images we capture are saved automatically. All thoughts and emotions – both negative and healthy – are involuntarily saved by the AMR phenomenon.

The bonds define the quality of the relationship

What do your children assimilate from you? Negative or positive images? All of them! They store your behaviors on a daily basis, whether wise or foolish. You may not realize it, but they are recording you at every moment.

The unconscious bonds are not only generated by what you say to them but also by what they see in you. Many parents say wonderful things to their children but have terrible reactions in front of them: they are intolerant, aggressive, biased, and deceitful. Over time, an emotional abyss is created between parents and children. Little affection, but many conflicts and criticisms.

Everything that is saved cannot be deleted, but can only be re-edited by new experiences upon old experiences. Re-editing is a possible yet complicated process. The image your child built of you can no longer be erased, only rewritten. Building an excellent image determines the richness of your relationship with your children.

Another important role of memory is that emotion defines the quality of what was recorded. All experiences with high emotional volume provoke a privileged recording. Love and hatred, joy and anguish triggers intense registration.

Without scientific expertise, the media discovered that emphasizing human misfortunes evokes emotion and concentration. In fact, accidents, deaths, diseases, and kidnappings generate a high level of tension, leading to a privileged filing of these images. Our memory has thus become like a dumpster. It is no wonder that the modern man is a restless individual, suffering in anticipation and afraid of the future.

Forgiving is cheaper

If you have an enemy, it's cheaper to forgive him. Do it for yourself. Otherwise, the AMR phenomenon will record it in a privileged manner. The enemy will sleep with you and disturb your sleep. Understand their weaknesses and forgive them, because only then, will you be free from them. Teach your children to make the stage of their mind a theater of joy, not a stage of terror. Lead them to forgive people who disappoint them. Explain this mechanism to them.

Our aggressions, rejections, and thoughtless attitudes can create a high level of emotional tension in our children, generating lasting scars. We need to understand how the unhealthy characteristics of personality are formed. The psychic mechanism works as follows: a painful experience is automatically recorded in the memory center. From there, it is continuously read, generating thousands of other thoughts. These thoughts are recorded again, generating the so-called conflict zones in the unconscious memory.

If you made a mistake with your child, simply being gentle with them again will not be enough. Worse, do not try to compensate for your aggressiveness by buying things for them. In this way, they will manipulate you and not love you. You will only fix your attitude and re-edit the unconscious film if you enter their world, recognize your overreaction, and talk to them about your attitude. Declare to your children that they are not on the footnotes of your life but on the main pages of your story.

In divorces, it is common for the father to promise the children that he will never abandon them. But when the guilt temperature drops, some parents also divorce their children. The children lose their presence, sometimes not physically but emotionally. Parents stop enjoying, smiling, praising and having pleasant moments with their children. When it happens, divorce raises great emotional repercussions. If the bridge is well built, if the relationship continues to be poetic and affective, the children will survive the turbulence of their parents' separation and will be able to mature.

Your children do not need giants

Individuality must exist because it is the foundation of the personality identity. There is no homogeneity in the learning process and the development of children (Vygotsky, 1987). There are no two identical people in the universe. But individualism is harmful. An individualistic person wants the world to revolve around their orbit; their satisfaction comes first, even if it implies the suffering of others.

Individualism among young people is exacerbated by parents' failure to connect their own and their children's stories. Even if you work a lot, make the most of your limited time available for amazing moments with your children. Roll on the carpet. Write poems. Play, smile, let go, and pleasantly tease them.

Once, a nine-year-old son asked his father, who was a doctor, how much he charged for a consultation. The father told him the amount. After a month, the son approached his father, showed some bills, emptied his coin bag and said to him with eyes full of tears, "Dad, I've been willing to talk to you for a long time, but you do not have time. I managed to save the amount for a consultation. Can you talk to me, please?"

Your children do not need giants; they just need human beings. They do not need executives, doctors, businessmen, company managers; they need you, just the way you are. Get into the habit of opening your heart to your children and letting them record an excellent image of your personality. Do you know what will happen next?

They will fall in love with you. They will take pleasure in spending time with you, in being close to you. Is there anything more enjoyable than this?

Financial crisis, losses, or hardships may strike your relationship, but if it has foundations, nothing can destroy it. On occasion, invite one of your children to join you for lunch or other activities. Tell them how important they are to you. Ask about their life. Talk about your work and challenges. Let your children be a part of your life. No psychological technique will work if love does not work.

If you go through a war at work but have peace when you get home, you will be a happy human being. But if you have joy outside home and live at war with your family, unhappiness will be your mate. Many children recognize the value of their parents but not enough to admire them, respect them, and consider them masters of life. Parents who have difficulties with their children should not feel guilty. Guilt stiffens the soul. In the human personality, nothing is definitive.

You can and should change this situation. You have extremely rich experiences, what makes your story more interesting than Hollywood films. If you doubt this, it's because you may not even know yourself and, worse, you may not even admire yourself. Release the happy child within you. Even if your hair has already turned gray, free the cheerful youthful self within your emotions. It is possible to recover the years. Let your children discover your world. Open yourself up, cry, and hug them. Crying and hugging are more important than giving them fortunes or heaping them with criticisms.

2

Good parents nourish the body; Brilliant parents nurture the personality

This habit of shining (or brilliant) parents contributes to developing: reflection, security, leadership, courage, optimism, overcoming fear, and preventing conflicts.

Good parents take care of the physical nutrition of their children. They encourage them to have a good diet with healthy, tender, and fresh foods. Brilliant parents go further: they understand that personality needs excellent emotional nutrition. They are concerned about the "foods" that promote intelligence and emotion.

In the past, a structured family guaranteed the development of a healthy personality in children. Today, good parents are witnessing their children becoming anxious, alienated, authoritarian, and distressed. Many children of doctors, judges, businessmen are going through serious conflicts. Why do intelligent and healthy parents watch their children become ill? Because society has become a stress factory.

We have no control over the process of shaping the personality of our children. We generate them and expose them to a controlling social system (Foucault, 1998) from an early age. They come into daily contact with thousands of enticing stimuli that infiltrate the matrices of their memory. For instance, parents teach their children to be supportive and consume only what is necessary, but the system teaches individualism and unnecessary consumption. Who wins this dispute? The social system does. The quantity of stimuli and emotional pressure the system exerts on the hearts of young people are intense. There is hardly any freedom of choice. Having culture, good financial conditions, an excellent marital relationship, and providing a good education for the youth is insufficient to promote mental wellness. An animal can only escape a predator's clutches with great skill. Prepare your children to survive on the turbulent waters of emotion and to develop critical thinking. Only then, can they filter out stressful stimuli and be free to choose and decide.

Parents who do not teach their children to be critical about advertisements, TV programs, and social discrimination make them easy targets for the predatory system. In this system, no matter how ethical it claims to be, your child is only a potential consumer and not a human being. Prepare your child to "be", because the world will prepare them to "have".

Feed their intelligence

Good parents teach their children how to brush their teeth; brilliant parents teach them how to maintain mental hygiene. Many parents beg their children daily to practice oral hygiene. But what about emotional hygiene? What is the use of preventing cavities if a child's emotion becomes a dumpster of negative thoughts, compulsions, fears, impulsive reactions, and social appeals?

Please teach the youth to protect their emotions. Everything that directly affects the emotions dramatically affects their memory and will shape their personality. Once, an excellent jurist told me in the office that if he had known how to protect his emotions from a young age, his life would not have been a drama. He had been rejected as a child by someone close because of a facial disfigurement. Rejection controlled his joy. His defect wasn't significant, but the AMR phenomenon recorded and perpetuated it. He had no childhood. He used to hide from people, living alone in the middle of the crowd. Help your children not to be enslaved by their problems. Feed with courage and boldness their theater of thoughts and the territory of their emotions. Do not settle if they are timid and insecure.

The Self, which represents conscious will (or the freedom to decide) must be trained to become a leader and not a puppet. Being a leader does not mean having the ability to solve everything and take on all the problems around us. Problems will always exist. If solvable, we have to solve them. On the other hand, if we cannot solve them, we need to accept our limitations. However, we should never get stuck in their orbit. If you had the ability to enter the stage of the young people's minds, you would find that many are tormented by anxious thoughts. Some are troubled by school exams, others by bodily aspects they dislike. Some think that nobody likes them. Many young people have poor self-esteem. Joy dies when low self-esteem is born.

Once, a sixteen-year-old boy came to me after a lecture. He stated that his peace was disrupted on a daily basis by worrying about growing old and dying. He was just beginning life, but he was disturbed by its end. How many young people are suffering without their parents or teachers even prying into their hearts? The emotional prison has incarcerated millions of young people. They suffer in silence. After closing this book, talk to them.

What kind of education is this, that talks about the world we live in but remains silent about the world we are? Always ask your children: "What's happening to you?" "Do you need me?" "Have you experienced any disappointment?" "What can I do to make you happier?"

What's the use of taking care of the daily nutrition of billions of cells in your children but neglecting their emotional nutrition? What's the use of having a healthy body if you are unhappy, unstable, lack emotional safety, run away from problems, fear criticism, and do not know how to accept "no" as an answer? No parent in the world would feed their children spoiled food, but we do this concerning emotional nutrition. We do not realize that everything they store in their memory will control their personalities.

Feed your children's personality with wisdom and tranquility. Talk about your adventures, moments of hesitation, emotional valleys you have crossed. Do not let the soil of their memory become a land of nightmares, but instead, a garden of dreams.

Do not forget that we trip on small stones and not on mountains. Small stones in the unconscious mind become large hills.

Pessimism is a cancer in the soul

You may not have money, but if you are rich in common sense, you will be a brilliant parent. If you influence your children with your dreams and enthusiasm, life will be uplifted. If you are an expert at complaining, demonstrating fear of life, fear of the future, and excessive worry about illnesses, you are about to paralyze their intelligence and emotions. Do you know how long an emotional conflict, without treatment and without genetic background, takes for spontaneous remission? Sometimes it takes three generations.

For example, if a father has an obsession with illnesses, one of the children may continuously record and reproduce this obsession. The grandson may have it with less intensity. Only the great-grandson may be free from it. Those who study the roles of memory know the gravity of the process of transmitting emotional illnesses.

Show strength and security to your children. Tell them frequently: "True freedom is within you," "Do not be frail in the face of your concerns," "Confront your quirks and anxiety," "Choose to be free! Every negative thought must be fought against to avoid being recorded." True optimism is built by facing problems, not by denying them. That is why motivational speeches rarely work. They do not provide tools to generate solid optimism that nourishes the "Self" as the leader of the theater of intelligence. Hence, the line of this book is scientific dissemination. My goal is to provide tools. According to research in American universities, an optimistic person has a 30% lower chance of having heart disease. Optimists have even less chance of having emotional and psychosomatic illnesses.

Pessimism is a cancer in the soul. Many parents are sellers of pessimism. It is not just the social garbage that the media deposits on the stage of young minds; many parents are also transmitting a gloomy future to them. Everything seems to be difficult and dangerous for them. They are preparing their children to fear life, to close themselves in a shell, to live without poetry. Nourish your children with solid optimism!

We should not create supermen, as Nietzsche advocated. Brilliant parents do not create heroes, but human beings who know their limits and their strength.

3

Good parents correct mistakes; Brilliant parents teach how to think

This habit of brilliant parents contributes to developing: critical awareness, thinking before reacting, loyalty, honesty, the ability to question, and social responsibility.

Good parents correct flaws; brilliant parents teach their children to think. Between correcting errors and teaching how to think, there are more mysteries than our vain psychology can imagine. Do not be an expert in criticizing inappropriate behaviors; be an expert in making your children reflect. Old scolding and familiar sermons definitely do not work; they only strain the relationship.

When you open your mouth to repeat the same things, you trigger an unconscious mechanism that opens certain memory files containing old criticisms. Your children will already know everything you are going to say. They will arm and defend themselves. Consequently, what you say will not resonate within them, will not generate an educational moment. This process is unconscious.

When your child makes a mistake, they already expect a reaction from you. If what you say does not impact their emotion, the AMR phenomenon will not produce an intelligent record, and consequently, there will be no growth, only suffering. Do not insist on repeating the same things for the same mistakes, for the same stubbornness. Sometimes, we insist for years on end, saying the same things, and young people keep repeating the same mistakes. They are stubborn, and we are foolish. Educating is not repeating words; it is creating ideas, enchanting. The same mistakes deserve new approaches.

If our children were computers, we could repeat the same procedure to correct the same error. But they have a complex intelligence. Daily, at least four phenomena read the memory and, among billions of options, they produce thousands of thought chains and countless transformations of emotional energy. It is not the purpose of this book to study the four phenomena that read the memory; I will just mention them: the memory trigger; the memory window; the autoflow; and the "Self," representing the conscious will.

The personalities of children and young people are in constant turmoil because the construction of thoughts never stops. It is impossible to stop thinking; even the attempt to interrupt thoughts is already a thought. Even while sleeping, we do not interrupt our thoughts, that is why we dream. Thinking is inevitable, but excessive thinking, as we will study, generates a violent drain of brain energy, drastically affecting our quality of life.

Do not be a rulebook

Computers are poor contraptions compared to the intelligence of any kid, even the special ones. Yet, we have been insisting on educating our children as if they were logical devices that only need to follow a rulebook. Every young person is a world to be explored. Rules are good for fixing computers. Saying "do this" or "do not do that" without explaining the causes, without stimulating the art of thinking, produces robots, not thinking young people. I believe that 99% of parents' criticisms and corrections are useless; they do not influence the personalities of young people. In addition to not educating, they generate more aggression and distance. So, what to do? Surprise them!

Brilliant parents understand how the mind works to better educate. They understand that they must first overcome the territory of the children's emotions, then the theater of their thoughts, and last the conscious and unconscious grounds of their memory, which is the box of secrets of their personality. Those parents surprise emotion with unique gestures. In this way, they generate fantastic educational moments.

Parents can read my theory, Piaget's ideas, Freud's psychoanalysis, Gardner's multiple intelligences, Plato's philosophy for decades; yet if they cannot enchant, teach to think, and conquer the warehouse of their children's memory, no study will have applicability and validity.

Surprising children is saying things they do not expect, reacting differently to their mistakes, exceeding their expectations. For example: if your child just raised their voice to you, what could you do? They expect you to shout and punish them. Instead, you initially remain silent, relax, and then say something that astonishes them: "I didn't expect you to offend me like that. Despite the pain you caused me, I love and respect you a lot." After saying these words, the parent exits the scene and allows the child think. The father's response will shake the foundations of their aggressiveness.

If you want to make a huge impact on the emotional and rational universe of your children, use creativity and sincerity. You will conquer the unconquerable. If you apply these principles at work, be sure that you will involve even the most complicated colleagues. However, you will not achieve conquest with a single gesture, but rather with a life agenda.

If you educate the emotional intelligence of your children with praise when they expect a scolding (Goleman, 1996), with encouragement when they expect an aggressive reaction, with an affectionate attitude when they expect an outburst of anger, they will be deeply moved and will remember you with greatness. Parents will thus become agents of change.

Good parents say to their children, "You are wrong!" Brilliant parents say, "What do you think about your behavior?" Good parents say, "You failed again!" Brilliant parents say, "Think before reacting." Good parents punish their children when they fail, while brilliant parents encourage them to see every tear as an opportunity for growth.

The "emotional hamburger" generation

Youth has always been a phase of rebellion against adult conventions. But the current generation has achieved a unique feat in history: it killed the art of thinking and the ability to question in youth. Young people rarely question adult behavior. Why is that so?

Because they love the poison we produce. They love quick success, immediate pleasure, the media spotlight, even if they live in anonymity. Excessive stimulation has generated a floating emotion without contemplative capacity. Even their life models must have explosive success. They want to be characters like artists or athletes who gain fame and applause overnight.

Young people live in the era of the "emotional hamburger." They detest patience.

They do not know how to admire the beauty in the little things of life. Do not ask them to admire flowers, sunsets, simple conversations. Everything is boring to them. Criticisms from parents and teachers are unbearable; they rarely listen to them attentively.

So, how to help them? Step out of the commonplace. One of the most important things in education is to lead a child to admire their educator. A father can be a handyman, but if he enchants his child, he will be great within them. A father can be great in the business world, or have thousands of employees, but if he does not captivate his child, he will be small in their soul.

Be a master of intelligence; teach them how to think. Let them capture the brilliant person you are. Will this plea find an echo?

4

Good parents prepare their children for success; Brilliant parents prepare them for failure

> *The ability to generate and seize opportunities, as well as motivation, boldness, patience, determination, and resilience, are all aided by this brilliant parents' habit.*

Good parents prepare their children to receive applause; brilliant parents prepare them to face their defeats. Good parents educate the logical intelligence of their children; brilliant parents educate their sensitivity.

Encourage your children to have goals, to seek success in study, work, and social relationships, but do not stop there. Lead them not to fear their failures. There is no podium without defeats. Many do not climb the podium, not because they lack the ability, but because they did not know how to overcome their failures on the way. Many cannot excel in their work because they gave up at the first obstacles. Some did not succeed because they lacked patience to endure a "no"; they lacked boldness to face some criticisms, and lacked humility to recognize their mistakes.

Perseverance is as important as intellectual ability. Life is a long road with unpredictable curves and inevitable skids. Society prepares us for days of glory, yet the days of frustration are the ones giving meaning to that glory.

Revealing maturity, brilliant parents place themselves as role models for a victorious life. For them, success is not like having a flawless life. Winning is not always getting it right. Therefore, they can tell their children: "I was wrong," "I'm sorry," "I need you." They are strong in convictions but flexible in admitting their weaknesses. Brilliant parents show that the most beautiful flowers emerge after the harshest winter.

Life is a risk contract

Parents who do not have the courage to admit their mistakes will never teach their children to face their own mistakes and grow from them. Parents who assume they are always right will never teach their children to transcend their failures. Parents who do not apologize will never teach their children to deal with arrogance. Parents who keep their fears hidden will always struggle to teach their children to perceive setbacks as opportunities to be stronger and more experienced. Have we been acting this way with our children, or are we just performing the trivial duties of education?

Living is a risk contract. Young people need to live this contract by appreciating challenges and not avoiding them. If they are intimidated by defeats or difficulties, the AMR phenomenon will register in their memory thousands of experiences that will fund the inferiority complex, low self-esteem, and a sense of incapacity. What is the consequence?

A young person with low self-esteem will feel diminished, inferior, without the ability to take risks and turn their goals into reality. They may experience premature emotional aging. Youth should be the best time for pleasure, despite its concerns. However, many are old people in young bodies. Being elderly does not mean being an old person. In fact, many elderly people, being happy and motivated, are younger in their emotions than many young people today. What is the characteristic of an aged emotion, without spice or motivation? It is the inability to contemplate beauty and an intense ability to complain, because nothing satisfies for long. Many complain about the body, clothes, friends, lack of money, school, and even for being born.

The ability to complain is the fertilizer for emotional poverty, and the ability to be grateful is the fuel for happiness. Many young people do plenty of things to have a hint of joy. They beg for the bread of joy, even though living in palaces. Young people who become masters of complaining have a great competitive disadvantage. They will hardly conquer social and professional space. Warn them! To help young people understand what human memory is, compare it to computer memory: Tell them that every complaint is accompanied by a high degree of tension, which, in turn, undergoes privileged filing by the AMR phenomenon in the memory, which slowly destroys the joy of emotion. The best years of life are suffocated. Little by little, they lose their smile, determination, and motivation.

Discovering the greatness of anonymous things

Lead your children to find great reasons to be happy in small things. Emotionally superficial people need big events to find pleasure, while deep people find pleasure in hidden things, in seemingly imperceptible phenomena: the movement of clouds, the butterflies' dance, a friend's hug, a lover's kiss, a look of complicity, the sympathetic smile of a stranger.

Happiness is not a matter of chance; it takes training. Train children to be excellent observers. Go through fields or gardens with them, make them observe a flower blooming, and discover the invisible beauty with them. Feel the beautiful things around you with your eyes. Lead young people to see the simple moments, the strength that arises in losses, the security that sprouts in chaos, the greatness that emanates from small gestures. Mountains are formed by hidden grains of sand.

Children will be happy if they learn to contemplate the beauty in both moments of glory and in failure, in the flowers of spring as well as in the dry leaves of winter. This is the great challenge of emotional education! For many, happiness is the madness of psychologists, the delirium of philosophers, the hallucination of poets. They have not understood that the secrets of happiness are hidden in simple and anonymous things, so distant and yet so close to them.

5

Good parents talk;
Brilliant parents engage in conversation as friends

This habit of brilliant parents contributes to developing: solidarity, companionship, zest for life, optimism, and interpersonal intelligence.

We have seen that the first habit of brilliant parents is letting their children know them; the second is nurturing their personalities; the third is teaching them to think; the fourth is preparing them for life's defeats and hardships. Now, we need to understand that the best way to develop all these habits is to acquire a fifth habit: dialogue.

Good parents talk; brilliant parents engage in dialogue. There is a vast difference between talking and engaging in dialogue. Talking is discussing the world around us; dialogue is discussing the world within us. It is sharing experiences, revealing what is hidden in our hearts, going beyond the curtain of behavior, and developing interpersonal intelligence (Gardner, 1995). Most educators cannot cross that curtain. According to a survey I carried out in São Paulo State (Brazil), over 50% of the parents have never had the courage to dialogue with their children about their fears, losses, and frustrations.

How is it possible for parents and children to live under the same roof for years and remain in total isolation? They claim to love each other, but invest little energy in nurturing that love. They are attentive to fixing cracked walls and car problems but neglect emotional cracks and relationship issues.

If a single faucet is leaking, parents worry about fixing it. However, do they take the time to have conversations with their children in order to assist them in restoring any joy, security, or sensibility that is slipping away? If we took all the money from a company and threw it in the trash, we would be committing a serious crime against it. It would go bankrupt. Have we not committed this crime against the most fascinating social enterprise – the family – whose only currency is dialogue? If we destroy dialogue, how will the parent-child relationship sustain itself? It will go bankrupt.

We need to establish a routine of conversing with our kids once a week at the very least. We must give them the freedom to talk about themselves, their concerns, and their relationships difficulties with siblings and us, their parents. You cannot imagine what these meetings can provoke.

If parents have never shared their most important dreams with their children, and have never heard from them about their greatest joys and most significant disappointments, they will become a group of strangers, not a family. There is no magic formula for building a healthy relationship. Yet dialogue is irreplaceable.

Looking for Friends

Every young person, no matter how complex or isolated they may be, has a world within to be discovered. Many young people are aggressive and rebellious, and their parents do not realize that they are shouting through their conflicts. Inappropriate behaviors are often silent cries begging for parental presence, affection, and attention. Many psychosomatic symptoms, such as headaches or abdominal pain, are also silent cries from children. Who is listening to them? Many parents take their children to psychologists, which can help, but ultimately, what the children are seeking is their parents' hearts.

Here is a suggestion: if you can, turn off regular TV and stick to cable. You will probably be amazed by how much better your kids' relationships with you and their siblings will be, once you take this step. They will be more affectionate, engage in more dialogues, have more time to play and have fun. They will watch fewer sensational channels and more contemplative ones that focus on nature and science.

For those without cable, here is an even more important suggestion than the first one – I call it the "Emotional Education Project" (EEP): every two months, spend a full week without watching TV and spend time doing interesting activities with your children instead. Plan to spend six weeks every year with them. Even if it is not possible to travel to distant destinations, parents and children should journey into each other's worlds. Make plans on what you will do. Go to the kitchen together, create new dishes, tell jokes, perform a family play, plant flowers, discover interesting things. Spend every night with your children during each of these weeks. Make the EEP a life project.

Parents' ultimate wish should be for their children to grow up to be their friends: diplomas, money and success are consequences of brilliant education. I have three daughters. As a father I will be frustrated if they do not become my friends, even though I am a well-known writer throughout the world.

Despite being a specialist in psychological conflicts, I also make mistakes, quite often. But knowing what to do with the mistakes is what matters. They can either build or destroy the relationship. I have apologized to my daughters on multiple occasions when I acted rashly, made hasty judgments, or raised my voice excessively. They were able to learn from me how to apologize and to acknowledge their own mistakes in this way.

Some people who witnessed me taking this approach were impressed. They said, "Cury is apologizing to his daughters?" They had never seen a father admit mistakes and apologize, especially a psychiatrist. Conflicts frequently arise among the children of psychologists and psychiatrists because their parents fail to relate to them on a human level, win their admiration, and speak to their hearts.

I do not want daughters to be afraid of me; I want them to love me. Fortunately, they are passionate about me and my wife. If there is love, obedience is spontaneous and natural. There is nothing more beautiful, more poetic, than parents being great friends to their children.

The Pearl of the Heart

Embracing, kissing, and spontaneously talking to children cultivates affection and breaks the bonds of loneliness. Many European and American people suffer from profound loneliness. They do not know how to touch their children and openly communicate with them. They live in the same house but exist in different worlds. Touching and dialoguing are magical: they restore purpose to existence, enrich emotion, and create a zone of solidarity. Because there is rarely someone who will enter their world and listen to them without prejudice, many young people in developed countries commit suicide. There is a misconception in psychiatry about suicide. Those who commit suicidal acts wish to end their suffering, not life.

Fundamentally, all people contemplating death have a hunger and thirst for life. What they seek to eradicate is the suffering brought on by their conflicts, the loneliness that cripples them, and the anguish that weakens them. When you convey this to those who are depressed, you will watch hope blossom within them. In my experience, I have helped many patients find the courage to change the course of their lives by saying these words to them. Some entered the office consumed by suicidal ideation but came out convinced that they desperately loved living.

In a society where parents and children are not friends, depression and other emotional disorders find an ideal environment to grow. Parental authority and respect from their children are not incompatible with the simplest friendship. On the one hand, you should not be permissive or a pawn in your children's hands; on the other hand, you should strive to be great friends with them.

We are in the era of admiration. Either your children admire you, or you will not have influence over them. True authority and genuine respect arise through dialogue. Dialogue is a hidden pearl in the heart. It is so precious and yet so accessible. Precious because gold and silver cannot buy it; accessible because even the poorest men can find it. Seek it.

6

Good parents provide information; Brilliant parents tell stories

> *This habit of brilliant parents contributes to developing: creativity, inventiveness, insight, schematic reasoning, and the ability to solve problems under pressure.*

Good parents are an encyclopedia of information; brilliant parents are pleasant storytellers. They are creative, insightful, capable of extracting beautiful life lessons from the simplest things. Do you want to be brilliant parents? So, develop the habit of telling stories in addition to just conversing. Captivate your children with your intelligence and affection, not with your authority, money, or power. Become pleasant ones. Influence the environment in which they are. Are you aware of the thermometer that shows if you are pleasant, indifferent, or unbearable? The image that your friends' children have of you does this work. If they enjoy being with you, you have passed the test. If they avoid you, you have failed and need to reconsider your attitudes.

I have always been a storyteller. My teenage daughters always asked me to tell them stories. Parents who are storytellers are not ashamed of using their mistakes and difficulties to help their children reach into themselves and find their ways. When children are in a desperate situation, fearing the future, or feeling apprehensive about confronting a problem, these parents intervene and tell stories that help turn the kids' nervous feelings into a source of motivation.

One of my children was once criticized by other girls for being simple, not appreciating ostentation, and not sharing their obsessive care for appearance. She felt rejected and sad. After listening to her, I set my imagination free and told her a story. I told her that some people prefer a beautiful sun painted in a picture, while others prefer a real sun, even if the clouds are covering it. I asked her: "Which sun do you prefer?" She thought about it and chose the real sun.

Then I added: "Even if people do not believe in your sun, it is still shining. You have your own light. One day, the clouds covering it will dissipate, and people will see it. Do not be afraid of others' criticism; be afraid of losing your light." She never forgot that story. She got so happy that she told it to several of her friends. Being happy is a training and not a work of chance. What is one of the most excellent ways of educating? Telling stories. Stories expand the world of ideas, freshen the emotion, and dissolve tensions.

The arrival of a new sibling can trigger aggressive reactions, rejections, instinctive regressions (e.g., loss of control over urination), and changes in attitude in the older sibling, damaging the development of their personality. Sometimes, the baby becomes a kind of "one that flew over the cuckoo's nest". Skilled parents create stories from the baby's gestation that include both siblings in fun experiences and encourage companionship. The older sibling considers these stories, stops seeing the younger one as a rival, and develops affection for them.

Teach a lot by talking little

The Master of masters was an excellent educator because He was a storyteller. Every parable shared by Him, two millennia ago, was a rich story that dismantled prejudices, broadened horizons, and encouraged critical thought. This was one of the secrets that explains why He was always surrounded by young people.

Young people appreciate intelligent individuals. You do not need to be a scientist or an intellectual to be intelligent; all you need to do is create stories and incorporate life lessons into them. Many parents are rigid in their thinking. They falsely believe that they lack insight, intelligence, and creativity – That is not true! As an intelligence researcher, I firmly believe that everyone has tremendous hidden intellectual potential.

I remember an autistic patient who couldn't produce any clear thoughts. His intellectual disability was significant. After using some tools that stimulated the AMR phenomenon, the windows of his memory opened. After two years of treatment, he was not only thinking brilliantly but also telling stories. All his classmates were astonished at his imagination. There is a storyteller within even the most reclusive and introspective human being.

How can you expect your children to listen to you, if there are moments when you yourself cannot stand your own closed-off manner? Do not shout, do not attack, do not retaliate aggressively. Stop! Tell stories to those you love. You can teach a lot by saying little. Be bold to change. Be inventive! You can educate a lot while expending little effort. Brilliant parents encourage their children to overcome their fears and live compassionate lives. They are storytellers, dream sellers. If you can make your children dream, you have the riches that many kings tried and failed to conquer.

7

Good parents give opportunities; Brilliant parents never give up

The development of the appreciation for life, hope, perseverance, motivation, determination, and the capacity to question oneself, to overcome obstacles and failures are all aided by this brilliant parent's habit.

Good parents are tolerant of some mistakes from their children; brilliant parents never give up on their children, even when they let them down and get emotional disorders. The world may not bet on our children, but we must never lose hope that they will become great human beings.

Brilliant parents are sowers of ideas and not controllers of their children. They sow in the soil of their intelligence and hope that one day their seeds will germinate. During the waiting period, there may be desolation, but if the seeds are good, they will germinate one day, even if the children do drugs, have no regard for life, and do not settle down for a career. Perhaps some parents are reading this book and crying. Their children are going through deep crises. They are unresponsive to the emotions of those who love them and refuse to receive treatment. What should you do? Give up on them? No, but act like the prodigal son's father.

The son gave up on the father, but the father never gave up on the son. The son left, but the father waited. Every day, the father hoped that his son would learn life lessons that he did not teach him directly. Finally, the great victory: anguish cracked the outer layer of the father's seeds and quietly molded the son's personality. He came back. Despite having severe scars on his soul, he is more experienced and mature. The father did not condemn the unjust son but threw a great party for him. No one understood. Love is incomprehensible.

We must be poets in the battle of education. We may cry, but never give up. We may get hurt, but never stop fighting. We must see what no one else sees: a treasure buried beneath stones of our children's hearts.

No one graduates from the task of educating

In the past, parents were authoritarian; today, the children are so. In the past, teachers were the students' heroes; today, they are their victims. Young people cannot stand being contradicted. Never before in history have children and young people dominated adults to such an extent. Children behave like kings whose desires must be immediately fulfilled.

First, learn how to say "no" to your children without being afraid. If they do not hear "no" from their parents, they will be unprepared to hear "no" from life. There is no way they can survive. Second, when it comes to saying "no," parents have to be firm against their children's demands and blackmail. Otherwise, children's and young people's emotions will become a seesaw: one moment docile, the next, explosive; one moment excited, the next, moody. They will be rejected in social environments if they are temperamental and blackmailers. Third, parents need to be clear regarding which boundaries are non-negotiable and which ones are negotiable. For example, staying up late during the week and having to wake up early to study is unacceptable and, therefore, non-negotiable. On the other hand, the amount of time on the Internet and the curfew time can be negotiated.

If parents adopt the behaviors of the exceptional teachers that I described, they will be able to set boundaries, contradict, and say "no" to their children without fear. Their grumbling, tantrums, and crises will not be destructive, but constructive. We live in challenging times. Rules and psychological advice seem to be ineffective. All throughout the world, parents feel helpless and unsuited to enter their children's worlds. Indeed, conquering our children's emotional planet is as complex as (or even more than) conquering the physical planet. Acting on the apparatus of intelligence is an art that few people learn.

I want to make it clear that the habits of brilliant parents reveal that no one graduates in the education of children. Those who say, "I know" or "I do not need anyone's help" have already been defeated. To educate, we must never stop learning in order to fully understand the meaning of the word "patience". Those who have no patience, give up; those who cannot learn, find no intelligent paths.

Unhappy are the psychiatrists who are unable to learn from their patients. Unhappy are the parents who are unable to learn from their children and rectify their courses. Unhappy are the teachers who are unable to learn from their students and update their tools. Life is a great school that provides little instruction for those who cannot read.

Because life is an excellent school, parents should strive to understand the habits of fascinating teachers that I will describe below. They will be useful on your journey. Teachers and parents work together as partners in the wonderful endeavor that is education.

PART 2

Seven Habits of Good Teachers...
and of those who are Fascinating Teachers

Educating is being a craftsperson of personality,
a poet of intelligence, a sower of ideas.

1

Good teachers are eloquent; Fascinating teachers understand the working of the mind

> *This fascinating habit helps students acquire the capacity to control their ideas, manage emotions, act as self-leaders, deal with setbacks and frustrations, and resolve conflicts.*

Good teachers have a solid academic culture and convey information confidently and eloquently in the classroom. Fascinating teachers go beyond this goal. They seek to understand the working of their students' minds to better educate. For them, every student in the classroom is more than just a number; students are complex human beings with individual needs.

Fascinating teachers transform information into knowledge and knowledge into experience. They are aware that only experience is registered in a privileged way on the soil of the memory and that only experience opens up pathways, in the memory, that have the power to transform personality. Therefore, they always turn the information into life experience.

Education is going through an unprecedented crisis in history. Students experience anxiety, alienation, lack of attention, and disinterest in their studies. Who is to blame for this? The students or the parents? Neither. The underlying causes are more profound and arise from the social system that frighteningly stimulated the thought building phenomena. We will study this subject in the following topic.

The stage of the minds of today's youth is not the same as it was in the past. The phenomena behind their minds, producing thoughts, are the same, but the actors on the stage are different. The quality and speed of thoughts have changed. To find the right instruments to turn education around, we must understand some of the roles played by the memory and some areas of the intelligence-building process.

The first habit of a fascinating teacher is to understand the student's mind and look for solutions that are unusual, different from what they are used to.

The ATS Syndrome

We are experiencing collective illness in this digital era. Despite its undeniable gains, the digital world has also caused an unprecedented disaster in the human brain, leading to changes in the dopamine and serotonin cycle, which generates dependence in the same level as cocaine. Digital addiction, especially in young people, is not a casual disorder, but a serious mental syndrome. Hundreds of millions of children, teenagers and adults present symptoms such as bad mood, restlessness, intolerance to frustration, self-demand, and deficits in empathy and in self-control; yet the most classic symptoms of this syndrome are a sense of urgency (the impulse of having everything quickly) and the aversion to boredom and loneliness, without knowing that these are fundamental elements for internalization and creativity.

Furthermore, every hour digital devices show more than sixty characters with a wide range of personality traits, such as irreverent police officers, fearless criminals, serial killers, all as funny people. These images are recorded in the memory and compete with the perceptions of parents and teachers. The unconscious consequences are serious. Educators lose the ability to influence the emotional world of young people. Their gestures and words lack emotional impact and, consequently, do not undergo privileged archiving capable of producing thousands of other emotions and thoughts that stimulate the development of intellect.

The most significant consequence of the excess stimuli from the screens is contributing to the generation of Accelerated Thinking Syndrome (ATS). We should never have tampered with the flight recorder of intelligence, which is the thought-building, but unfortunately, we did. The speed of thoughts should not be increased chronically. Otherwise, there would be a decrease in concentration and an increase in anxiety. That is precisely what is happening with young people today.

ATS anxiety generates a compulsion for new stimuli, in an effort to alleviate it. Although less intense, the principle is the same as in psychological drug dependence. Drug abusers always use new doses to try to relieve the anxiety generated by the dependence. The more they use, the more dependent they become. ATS carriers develop a dependence on new stimuli. They fidget on their chairs, have parallel conversations, cannot concentrate, and bother their peers. All these behaviors are attempts to alleviate the anxiety generated by ATS.

We unintentionally committed a crime against the minds of children and adolescents, which has resulted in a bankrupt education system, increasing violence, and social alienation. I have scientific conviction that the speed of young people's thoughts a century ago was much lower than it is now, and for this reason, despite its limitations, the previous educational approach was effective. We need a new education model. At the end of this book, I will go over ten techniques for creating excellent education that can deal with ATS's negative effects.

During my lectures, when I ask teachers, who have been teaching for over a decade, if they think that students nowadays are more agitated than those in the past, the unanimous answer is affirmative. We need extraordinary teachers who understand the theater of the human mind. The world is full of ordinary teachers. Thinking is excellent, but thinking too much is terrible. Excessive thinking drains crucial energy from the cerebral cortex, causing excessive fatigue, even without physical activity. This is one of the symptoms of ATS.

Other symptoms include insufficient sleep, irritability, suffering from anticipation, forgetfulness, concentration deficit, aversion to routine, and occasionally psychosomatic symptoms, such as headaches, muscle aches, tachycardia and gastritis. Why is forgetfulness one of the symptoms? Because the brain, being more sensible than we are, blocks memory to reduce excessive thinking and conserve energy.

Many scientists do not realize that ATS is the main cause of the crisis in global education. It is collective, affecting large part of the adult and child population. Responsible adults have a stronger ATS and, therefore, are more stressed. Why is that so? Because they work in an intellectually demanding field, think more deeply, and show greater concern.

ATS in students means that the past educational and psychological theories have little result, because while teachers speak, students are restless, unfocused, without concentration, and, moreover, traveling in their thoughts. Teachers are present in the classroom, and students are in another world.

Causes of ATS

The ATS syndrome generates non-genetic hyperactivity. Since the dawn of humanity, genetic hyperactivity has always existed, characterized by psychomotor anxiety, restlessness, and agitation of thought from a metabolic background. That is why some people have always been more anxious, stubborn, and hyper-thinking than others. However, today there is a non-genetic functional hyperactivity – the ATS.

What are the causes of ATS? As I mentioned before, firstly, is the overabundance of auditory and visual stimuli from the screens, which directly impacts the emotion domain. Notice that I am not talking about the quality of the contents but the excess of stimuli, whether they are good or terrible. Secondly, is the excess of information. Thirdly, the paranoia of consumption and aesthetics, which hinders internalization. All these factors stimulate the thought-building and generate psycho-adaptation to daily routine stimuli, that is, a loss of pleasure in the small things of everyday life. ATS carriers are constantly anxious, searching for a stimulation to ease their discomfort.

When it comes to information overload, it's important to remember that a child today, at the age of seven, has access to more information in their memory than a person at the age of seventy, one or two centuries ago. This avalanche of information improperly stimulates the four great phenomena that read memory and build thought chains. Those with ATS cannot fully manage thoughts or calm their minds.

The greatest villain of modern man's quality of life is not his work, competition, excessive working hours, or social pressures, but the excess of thoughts. ATS impacts mental health in three ways: ruminating on the past and developing feelings of guilt, producing concerns about existential problems, and suffering in anticipation. It is not enough to be eloquent. Being a fascinating teacher requires understanding the human soul to discover pedagogical strategies that turn the classroom and home into an oasis rather than a source of stress. For both teachers and students, it is a question of survival; without it, their quality of life will be diminished. And this is already happening.

The teacher's quality of life has been destroyed

Now, look at a shocking revelation: In Spain, 80% of teachers are stressed. In England, the government is struggling to train teachers, especially in elementary and secondary education, because few want this profession. In other countries, the situation is equally critical. According to research by the Academy of Intelligence Institute, in Brazil, 92% of teachers have three or more stress symptoms, and 41% have ten or more of that. It is an extremely high number, which indicates that almost 1/2 of the teachers should not be in the classroom, but admitted to an anti-stress nursing home. Compare this with another number: among the dramatically stressed population of São Paulo City, 22.9% have ten or more symptoms.

The numbers stand out. They indicate that teachers are almost twice as stressed as the population of São Paulo, which is one of the largest and most stressful cities in the world. In my opinion, every developed country faces the same situation. The symptoms that stand out the most are related to the accelerated thinking syndrome.

What sort of war is it that we are engaged in if our brave warriors on the front lines – the teachers – are collectively falling ill? What kind of education are we building that is eliminating the good quality of life of our dear teachers? We value the markets of oil, car, and computer, but we do not realize that the intelligence market is failing. Not only do teachers' salaries and dignity need to be rescued, but also their health. Teachers and students collectively have ATS.

A plea to fascinating teachers: please, be patient with your students. They are not guilty for the hostility, alienation, or restlessness that is occurring in the classroom. They are victims. There is a world waiting to be explored and discovered behind the most challenging students.

There is hope in chaos. We need to build the school of our dreams. Hold on!

2

Good teachers have methodology; Fascinating teachers have sensitivity

This practice of fascinating teachers helps students develop their self-esteem, stability, tranquility, the ability to contemplate beauty, the ability to forgive, to make friends, and to socialize.

Good teachers speak with their voice; fascinating teachers speak with their eyes. Good teachers are didactic; fascinating teachers go beyond: they have sensitivity to speak to the hearts of their students.

Be a fascinating teacher. Speak with a voice that expresses emotion. Change your tone while speaking. Thus, you will captivate emotion, stimulate concentration, and alleviate the ATS of your students. They will slow their thoughts down and travel in the world of your ideas. A fascinating math, chemistry, or language teacher is someone who can lead their students on a journey without leaving the classroom. Every time I give a lecture, I try to make my listeners travel, reflect on life, walk within themselves, leave the common place.

A fascinating teacher is a master of sensitivity. They know how to protect the emotion in moments of tension. What does that mean? It means not letting the aggression and thoughtless attitudes of their students steal their tranquility. They understand that the weak ones exclude, while the strong welcome; the weak condemn, yet the strong ones understand. They try to accept and comprehend all of their students, even the most difficult ones.

See the world through the eyes of an eagle. Look at education from various angles. Understand that we are creators and victims of the social system that values having instead of being; looks instead of content; consumption instead of ideas. As far as it depends on us, we must do our share to generate a healthier mankind.

Do not forget that you are not just a pillar of the classical school but a pillar of the school of life. Be aware that computers can generate giants in science but children in maturity. Notwithstanding these challenges, educators are irreplaceable, because kindness, solidarity, tolerance, inclusion, altruistic feelings, in short, all areas of sensitivity, cannot be taught by machines, but by human beings.

3

Good teachers educate logical intelligence; Fascinating teachers educate emotion

> *This habit of fascinating teachers contributes to the development of security, tolerance, solidarity, perseverance, emotional and interpersonal intelligence, protection against stressful stimuli.*

Good teachers teach their students to explore the world around them, from the vastness of space to the tiny atom. Fascinating teachers teach students to explore the world they are, their own being. Their education follows the chords of emotion.

Fascinating teachers know that working with emotion is more complex than working with the most intricate calculations in physics and mathematics. Emotion can transform the rich into beggars, intellectuals into children, and powerful individuals into fragile beings. Educate the emotion intelligently. Yet, what is educating emotion? It is stimulating the student to think before reacting, not to fear, to be a self-leader, the author of one's own story, to know how to filter stressful stimuli, and to work not only with logical facts and concrete problems, but also with the contradictions of life.

Educating emotion is also giving without expecting something in return, being true to one's conscience, deriving pleasure from the small stimuli of existence, to stand losing, taking risks to turn dreams into reality, having the courage to walk through unknown places. Who had the privilege of educating emotion in their youth? Unfortunately, we enter society unprepared for life. We are vaccinated from childhood against a series of viruses and bacteria, but we do not receive any vaccine against disappointments, frustrations, and rejections. How many tears, mental illnesses, relationship crises, and even suicides could be avoided with emotional education?

Without emotional education, we tend to generate at least three results: Some become insensitive, with traits of a psychopathic personality. They have an insensitive emotion, they injure and insult people because they lack empathy, yet they are indifferent to pain and do not consider the repercussions of their actions. Others, on the contrary, become hypersensitive. They intensely live the pain of others, give themselves without limits, worry too much about others' criticism, they have no emotional protection. An insult ruins the day, the month, and even life. Hypersensitive people are usually excellent to others but terrible to themselves.

Others remain alienated, they do no harm to others, yet instead of planning for the future, they have no dreams, no goals, they just let it go and live an unhealthy conformity. Schools are failing to educate emotion. They have been producing young people who are insensitive, hypersensitive, or alienated. We need to educate young people who have a rich, protected, and integrated emotion.

4

Good teachers use the memory as information storage; Fascinating teachers use it as a foundation for the art of thinking

> *This habit of fascinating teachers helps to develop: critical sense, thinking before reacting, exposing ideas rather than imposing them, debating, questioning, and teamworking.*

Good teachers use memory as a storehouse of information; fascinating teachers use it as foundation for creativity. Good teachers complete the course curriculum; fascinating teachers do so as well, yet their main objective is to develop critical thinking skills in their students rather than raising repeaters of information. Classic education has transformed human memory into a single database. Memory does not have this purpose. As I said, much of the information we receive will never be remembered. We occupy precious memory space with unimportant or even useless information.

Teachers and psychologists assure that there is recollection. However, as we have already said, this is one of the great myths on which psychology and education sciences are based. There is no pure recollection of the past, but a reconstruction of the past with micro or macro differences. How many thoughts did we produce yesterday? Thousands! How many can we recall with the precise combination of verbs, nouns, and adjectives? Perhaps none. But if we attempt to recall the people, settings, and situations we have related to, we will reconstruct hundreds of other thoughts that are not quite the same as the ones we had yesterday.

Then we conclude that the purpose of memory is not to provide support for mere recollection, but for the creative reconstruction of the past. Only logical knowledge, such as numerical values, is retained in pure recollection, devoid of social or emotional experiences. Even then, the recollection of these memories involves subtle underlying emotions. Because of this, our capacity to complete calculations varies depending on the situation.

The human memory demands creativity, yet traditional education demands repetition from the students. Unlike the computers, our memory is not a database, nor is our capacity for thinking a machine for repeating information. Computer memories are slaves to programmed stimuli. Human memory is a collection of knowledge and experiences that enable each of us to create an amazing world of ideas.

The intellectual potential of an African tribesman is equivalent to that of a Harvard scientist. Einstein is often regarded as the greatest intellectual of the 20th century. However, as one of the few scientists who has published research on the process of thought-building, I firmly believe that an Amazonian native tribesman possesses the same level of intellectual capacity as Einstein did. We all possess a set of phenomena that read the memory fields in milliseconds and generate the spectacle of thoughts. We just do not produce great ideas, unusual thoughts, surprising creations because we constrict the art of thinking.

I only had two copybooks for my first two years of high school, and very little was written in them. It was hard to adapt to an education that did not challenge my intelligence. Some people at the time believed I would never achieve anything in life because of my seeming lack of interest. But inside me, there was an explosion of ideas. Thinking was an adventure that enchanted me.

Today, I have more than five thousand pages written, and just a small percentage have been published. Scientists study my books and millions of people around the world read them. Nonetheless, I am certain that my intelligence is not privileged. We all have a special mind; The point we achieve depends on how much we free the art of thinking.

Opening the Windows of Intelligence

In addition to being ineffective, school exams that encourage students to repeat information are often detrimental because they suppress critical thinking. Exams should be open to interpretation, encouraging students' creativity, developing their capacity for independent thought, encouraging schematic reasoning, and expanding their capacity for reasoning. Multiple-choice questions and quizzes should be avoided or used sparingly as assessments for education.

Exams should value any structured thought or schematic reasoning, even if it is completely unrelated to the subject matter. An "A plus" for brilliant reasoning based on incorrect data is possible. This values thinkers. The demand for details should not occur in elementary and high school; it should only be required from university specialists.

In my book "Revolutionize Your Quality of Life", I talk about the Memory of Continuous Usage (or conscious memory) – MCU, and the Existential (or unconscious) Memory – EM. The vast majority of information, perhaps more than 90%, that we record in the MCU will never be remembered. They go to the periphery of memory, to the EM, and will be re-edited (replaced) or transferred to rarely-accessed files in the basements of the unconscious mind.

The most useful information are the ones converted into knowledge and, in turn, transformed into experiences in the MCU. When we talk about the school of our dreams, I will point out tools to stimulate the art of thinking. In the past, knowledge would double every two or three centuries. Currently, knowledge doubles every five years. However, where are the thinkers? We are witnessing the end of thinkers in schools, universities, and even in postgraduate courses. We have multiplied knowledge, but not thinkers.

Students who perform poorly on exams today may become excellent scientists, executives, and practitioners in the future. We just need to stimulate them. Encourage your students to open the windows of their minds, to have the audacity to think, to question, to debate, and to break paradigms. This is an excellent habit. Fascinating teachers shape thinkers who are authors of their own story.

5

Good teachers are temporary masters; Fascinating teachers are unforgettable ones.

> *This habit of fascinating teachers contributes to developing wisdom, sensitivity, affectivity, serenity, love for life, the ability to speak to the heart, and the ability to influence others.*

A good teacher is remembered during the school years. A fascinating teacher is an unforgettable master. A good teacher seeks out students; a fascinating teacher is sought after by them. A good teacher is admired; a fascinating teacher is loved. A good teacher cares about the students' grades; a fascinating teacher cares about turning them into engineers of ideas. Being an unforgettable master is shaping human beings who will make a difference in the world. Their life lessons have a permanent mark on their students' conscious and unconscious minds. Time may pass, and challenges may arise; however, the seeds of a fascinating teacher will never be destroyed.

    I have investigated the lives of great thinkers such as Confucius, Buddha, Plato, Freud, and Einstein. All of them were unforgettable masters because they stimulated their inner selves to sail inward. In the collection of books "An Analysis of The Intelligence of Christ" (Cury, 2000), I had the opportunity to investigate the thoughts of Jesus Christ, as well as His capacity to protect emotion and His ability to work on the soils of His disciples' intelligence.

Despite my limits, I examined His personality from a psychological point of view rather than a religious perspective. The results were extraordinary. Perhaps, for the first time, texts related to Jesus Christ have been adopted in psychology, pedagogy, and law faculties. Apparently, He died as the most defeated of men because the strongest of His disciples denied Him, and the others abandoned Him. But no one is defeated when their seeds are underground. He created a caste of brilliant thinkers out of unprepared Galilean young men by sowing seeds of intelligence, emotion, and breaking the fear-based jail system in their memory soils.

My conclusion is that Jesus Christ's legendary status arose from His exceptional ability to skillfully communicate to the human mind's theater, not from supernatural acts. Never before has someone so great humbled himself in order to elevate the humble to greatness. Those who love education should study him, regardless of religious views.

Excellent schools have generated students with problems. In the past, peripheral schools could not help their "problematic students". Today, good schools that use respectable theories, such as constructivism and multiple intelligences, have been unable to collectively form wise and lucid young people.

Be a fascinating master. Encourage your students to think critically and to overcome obstacles rather than merely adopting an informational mindset. Stimulate them to manage their thoughts and to have a love affair with life. Do not be silent about your story; share your life experiences. Information is saved in the memory; experiences are engraved in the heart.

6

Good teachers correct behavior; Fascinating teachers resolve conflicts in the classroom

> *This fascinating teaching habit helps students overcome anxiety, handle interpersonal conflicts, socialize, find emotional safety, and reclaim self-leadership in high-stress situations.*

Good teachers correct aggressive behaviors in students, while fascinating teachers resolve conflicts in the classroom. Resolving conflicts and correcting behaviors in the noble field of education are farther apart than one may think. Resolving conflicts in the classroom is a relatively new topic in many countries. Only now are some European countries and the USA awakening to this reality. For some time, I have been emphasizing at conferences that parents and teachers need to equip themselves to handle conflicts among their children and students.

First, as I already mentioned, it is important to comprehend the ATS syndrome. Second, in the heat of student conflicts, educators must protect their own emotions; otherwise, dissension can severely wear them down. In this case, the school will turn into a wilderness, and the teachers will count down the days left to retire. Third, the best response, when faced with dissensions, insults, or a crisis among students or between students and the teacher, is not to give any answer. In the first thirty seconds of tension, we make our worst mistakes, our worst atrocities. When things get tense, be friends with silence, and take a deep breath.

Why to use the tool of silence? Because tense emotion closes the territory of memory reading, obstructing the construction of thought chains. Thus, we react on instinct, like animals, and not with intelligence. Fourth, refrain from giving an aggressive person a lecture. This procedure has been used since the Stone Age and it does not work; it does not provide an educational moment because the aggressor's emotions are heated.

What could you do? Use the tool I mentioned when I talked about parents. Enchant your class with unexpected gestures. Surprise your students. This way, you will resolve conflicts in the classroom. How can it be? Lead them to think, to dive into themselves, to confront themselves. It's not an easy task, but it's possible. Let's see how it can be done.

A Gentle Slap Straight to the Heart

Once, some students were talking at the back of the classroom. The language teacher requested silence, but they continued chattering. She was more assertive and called attention to a student who was talking loudly. He responded aggressively, shouting: "You're not my boss! I pay for you to work!" Now, tension filled the air. Everyone expected the teacher to shout at the student or kick him out of class. Instead, she remained silent, relaxed, reduced her tension and freed her imagination. Then, she told them a story seemingly unrelated to the aggressive atmosphere.

She recounted the story of Jewish children and adolescents who were imprisoned in Nazi concentration camps, deprived of their rights. They could not go to school, play on the streets, visit friends, sleep in a warm bed, or eat with dignity. The food was spoiled, and they slept as if they were objects piled up in a warehouse. And what was worse: they could not hug their parents. The world had fallen on them. They cried, and no one consoled them. They were hungry, and no one fed them. They screamed for their parents, but no one heard them. In front of them there were only dogs, guards, and barbed wire fences. The teacher described what was one of the worst crimes ever committed in our history. Human rights and the lives of those young people were stolen. Over a million children and adolescents died.

After telling this story, the teacher didn't need to say much. She looked at the class and said, "You have school, friends, teachers who love you, the affection of your parents, delicious food on your table, yet do you appreciate them?" She guided her students to consider the value of human rights and to put themselves in other people's shoes, in order to resolve problems in the classroom. She did not need to reprimand the student who had offended her. She knew that correcting his behavior would not work, and she wanted to make him a thinker. He fell completely silent. He went home and was never the same again because he understood that he had many beautiful things that he did not appreciate.

Parents and teachers are lost in the world of their classrooms. Teachers are confused inside the classroom. Parents lack direction in the "homeroom". We cannot accept that neither of these environments fosters meaningful life experiences for young people to learn.

Learn how to give gentle "slaps" to the heart of those you love. We need to awaken our children and young people for life. Affection and intelligence heal the wounds of the soul; rewrite the closed pages of the unconscious mind.

7

Good teachers prepare students for a profession; Fascinating teachers prepare them for life

This habit of fascinating teachers contributes to the development of solidarity, overcoming psychic and social conflicts, developing entrepreneurial spirit, the ability to forgive, filtering of stressful stimuli, decision-making, questioning, and goal-setting.

A good teacher educates their students for a profession, yet a fascinating teacher educates them for life. Fascinating teachers are revolutionary practitioners. No one knows how to measure their power, not even themselves. Just by preparing their students for life through the spectacle of ideas, they can change paradigms, alter the course of a people's history, and alter a societal structure without using weapons.

Fascinating masters may be despised and threatened, but their strength cannot be matched. They are "arsonists" who inflame society with the warmth of their intelligence, compassion, and simplicity. They are fascinating because they are free, and they are free because they think, and they think because they love life profoundly. Their students acquire an extraordinary asset: critical sense. Therefore, they are not manipulated, controlled, or blackmailed. They know what they want in a world of uncertainties.

Fascinating teachers are promoters of self-esteem. They pay particular attention to timid, disregarded students who receive offensive nicknames. They know these ones can be imprisoned by their traumas. Therefore, as poets of life, they reach out and reveal their inner potential to them. They encourage them to use pain as fertilizer for their growth. In this way, they prepare them to survive social storms.

Shaping Entrepreneurs

Fascinating teachers aim for their students to become leaders of themselves. They declare to their students in the classroom in numerous ways: "May you be great entrepreneurs. If you undertake, do not be afraid to fail. If you fail, do not be afraid to cry. If you cry, think again about your life, but keep going. Always give yourself another opportunity."

When hardships weigh on their students, when the nation's economy is in crisis or social issues are widespread, they will declare in their turn: "Losers only see the lightning. Winners see the rain, and with it, the opportunity to cultivate. Losers become motionless in the face of frustrations and losses. Winners see the opportunity to change everything again. Never give up on your dreams!"

Prepare your students to explore the unknown, to fear not failure but the regret of not trying. Teach students how to conquer innovative experiences by observing little adjustments and making significant route corrections. New stimuli establish a relationship with the previous cognitive structure, generating new experiences (Piaget, 1996). New experiences foster intellectual growth. Lead young people to recognize the value of flexibility in both work and life, since only those who are incapable of producing an idea will be unable to change their minds. Help them to learn a valuable lesson from each tear.

If we do not rebuild education, modern societies will become a large psychiatric hospital. Statistics show that being stressed is considered "normal", and "abnormal" is to be healthy.

PART 3

The Educator's Seven Deadly Sins

Everybody makes mistakes; the majority use them to destroy themselves, while a few people use them to strengthen themselves. Those are the wise ones.

1

Correcting in public

In education, correcting someone in public is the first capital sin. An educator should never expose a person's flaw in front of others, no matter how bad it is. Public exposure leads to humiliation and complex traumas that are hard to overcome. An educator should value the person who makes a mistake more than the mistake itself. Parents or teachers should only intervene publicly when a young person has offended or harmed someone in public. Even so, they should proceed cautiously to avoid escalating tensions.

There was a smart, intelligent, sociable twelve-year-old girl who was a bit overweight. Apparently, she had no issue with her weight and was a good, participative student, respected by her peers. One day, her life took a drastic turn: She failed a test. She went to the teacher and questioned her grade. The teacher, who was angry amidst other issues, dealt a fatal blow by referring to her as a "chubby not very smart" in front of her classmates. Correcting someone in public is serious; humiliating them is dramatic. The girl felt diminished, inferior, and cried, experiencing high levels of tension that were particularly registered in the Memory of Continuous Usage (MCU).

If we look at the memory as a big city, the original trauma produced by the teacher's humiliation was like a rotten shack situated in a beautiful neighborhood. The girl continuously read the file containing this trauma, producing thousands of negative thoughts and emotional reactions, which were recorded again, expanding the trauma's structure. Thus, a shack in memory can infect an entire file.

Contrary to what Freud believed, it is not the original trauma that becomes the greatest villain of mental health, but its feedback. That teenager would associate her experience to every hostile gesture from others. Over time, she created thousands of "rotten shacks". A once beautiful neighborhood in the unconscious mind turned into a desolate land. Teenagers should feel beautiful regardless of whether they are overweight, have a physical disability, or their bodies fail to meet the ideal of beauty dictated by the media. Beauty is in the eye of the beholder.

Unfortunately, the media has massacred young people, defining beauty in their unconscious minds. Every image of a model from TV shows, ads, and magazine covers is saved in memory and creates matrices that exclude those who do not fit that profile. This process imprisons young people, even the healthiest ones. When they stand in front of the mirror, what do they see? Their qualities or their flaws? Most often, their flaws. Young people are discriminated against by the seemingly harmless media in the same way that black people have historically and currently experienced discrimination.

Remember it is through this process that rejection turns into a monster, a strict teacher becomes an executioner, an elevator changes into an airless cubicle, and public humiliation paralyzes the intellect and creates fear of expressing ideas. The girl in our story increasingly obstructed her memory due to low self-esteem and a sense of inadequacy. She ceased achieving good grades, solidified a lie that she lacked intelligence, went through multiple depressive crises, lost interest in life, and attempted suicide when she was eighteen. Fortunately, she survived, sought treatment, and overcame that trauma. Deep down, she did not want to end her life; just as any depressive person, she was hungry and thirsty for life. Her desire was to eliminate her intense suffering, hopelessness, and inferiority complex.

Publicly drawing attention or pointing out a mistake or flaw in young people and adults can generate an unforgettable trauma that will control them throughout their lives. Even if young people disappoint you, please do not humiliate them. Even if they deserve a scolding, try to talk to them privately and then correct them. But, above all, encourage young people to reflect. Those who stimulate reflection are craftspeople of wisdom.

2

Expressing authority with aggressiveness

A son once confronted his father after becoming disappointed with his aggressive response. The father beat him after feeling confronted and ordering him never to talk to him that way ever again. By yelling, he asserted that he was the one in charge in that house, that he was the one supporting him. By instilling terror, this father imposed his authority with violence, but he permanently lost his son's love.

Many parents attack and criticize each other in front of their children. When we are anxious and unable to have a conversation, the best thing is to step back. Go to another room and do something else until you can open the memory windows and intelligently address controversial issues. However, there are no perfect couples. We all make mistakes in front of our children, and we all get stressed. Even the calmest person experiences moments of anxiety and irrationality. So, even though desirable, it is impossible to avoid all conflicts in front of children. What matters is how we respond to our mistakes.

The same principle applies to teachers. When we display aggressive behavior in front of the kids, we should apologize not only to our spouse but also to our children for witnessing our intolerance. If we have the courage to make mistakes, we should have the courage to correct them. An authoritarian person is not always ruthless and aggressive. Sometimes, their stubbornness and delicate immutability serve as a disguise for their aggression. Nobody changes their opinion. We will be guilty of a capital sin in our children's education if we insist on maintaining our authority at any costs. Our authoritarianism will control their intelligence.

In the future, our children may react the same way we did. In fact, notice that we often imitate our parents' behaviors that we most strongly disapproved of during our childhood. The unprocessed, silent record forms molds in our personality's innermost secrets. Some children will provoke their parents by pointing out their mistakes when they're irritated. Many parents lose their children's affection because they are unable to have a conversation with them when confronted. They are afraid that dialoguing will diminish their authority. They cannot handle being questioned. Some parents hate it when their children point out their mistakes. They feel like untouchable. They react with violence. Their imposition of power suppresses their children's lucidity. They are raising people who will also react with violence.

Parents who impose their authority are those who are afraid of their own weaknesses. Limits must be set but, in a general manner, not imposed. Some limits, as I previously mentioned, are non-negotiable since they jeopardize the children's well-being and safety. Even in these situations, though, a round-table discussion with children should take place to go over the reasons for these limitations.

In these twenty years of attending numerous patients, I have discovered that certain parents were extremely loved by their children. They did not provide them material possessions or social privileges, nor did they beat them or act in an authoritative manner. What was their secret? They committed themselves to their kids, helped them learn about emotions, and connected their own world with their children's world. Even without being aware of the principles I outlined for brilliant parents, they led a natural life.

Dialogue is an irreplaceable educational tool. In the relationships between parents and children, as well as between teachers and students, authority is necessary, but true authority is earned with intelligence and love. Parents who, from an early age, kiss, praise, and encourage their children to think, are not at risk of losing them or their respect.

We should not be afraid of losing our authority;
we should be afraid of losing our children.

3

Being overly critical: obstructing a kid's childhood

There was a father who was extremely concerned about his son's future. He wanted him to be ethical, serious, and responsible. The child was not allowed to make mistakes or indulge in excess. He was not allowed to play, get dirty, or act silly like other kids. He had lots of toys, but they were stored away because his mom and dad did not approve of mess. The father was quick to criticize his son's mistakes, poor grades, or foolish behavior. One critique was not sufficient; he often directed a series of criticisms at his son in front of his friends. His criticism was obsessive and unbearable. Furthermore, the father compared his son's actions to those of other young people in an effort to put pressure on him into correcting his behavior. The boy felt like he was despised by all. He was so certain that his parents did not love him, so that he considered giving up on life.

What was the result? The son grew up to be a good man. He made few mistakes, was serious, ethical, but unhappy, shy, and fragile. There was an abyss between him and his parents. Why? Because there was no appealing joy and spontaneity between them. The family was exemplary, though depressing and bland. The son not only became shy but frustrated. He feared the criticism of others. He was afraid of making mistakes, so he buried his dreams and avoided taking risks.

The father, in his desire to do the right thing, committed some capital sins in the course of his education. He imposed authority, humiliated his son in public, criticized him excessively, and obstructed his childhood. This father was prepared to fix computers, yet not to educate a human being. Every one of these capital sins is universal, as it is a problem in modern society just it was in primitive tribes.

Do not criticize excessively. Do not compare your child to their peers. Every young person is a unique being in the theater of life. Comparison is only educational if it is stimulating rather than demeaning. Give your children the freedom to have their own experiences, even if it includes certain risks, failures, foolish attitudes, and some suffering. Otherwise, they will not find their own paths.

Keeping young people in a greenhouse and preventing them from making mistakes or going through hardships is the worst way to prepare them for life. Greenhouses are good for plants, but human intelligence is suffocated by them. The Master of masters has important lessons to give us in this area. Even the most discerning scientists are enchanted by His educational attitudes. He once said that Peter would deny Him. Peter vehemently disagreed. Jesus could have criticized him, proven his flaws, or pointed out his fragility. But what did Jesus do? Nothing.

He did nothing to change his friend's ideas. He let the young apostle Peter have his experiences. What was the result? Peter made an awful mistake, cried uncontrollably, but learned unforgettable lessons. He might never have grown into the person he became if he had not made that mistake and recognized how fragile he was. However, he gained the ability to accept, forgive, and include others as a result of his failure. Dear educators, we must keep in mind that the weak ones condemn, yet the strong ones understand; the weak judge, but the strong forgive. However, it is impossible to be strong without acknowledging our own limitations.

4

Punishing when angry and setting limits without explanations

Once, an eight-year-old girl was walking in a shopping mall near her school with some friends. Spotting some money on a counter, she took it. The saleswoman saw it and called her a thief. She grabbed the girl by the arm and led her, in tears, to her parents. The parents were desperate. Some people nearby expected them to beat and punish their daughter. Instead, they asked me to advise them on how to handle that issue. They were afraid that the girl would become a kleptomaniac and take things that did not belong to her.

I advised the parents not to make a big deal out of that case. Children will always make mistakes; the key is knowing how to handle them. My concern was not to punish their sweet girl; rather, I was trying to help them win her back. I suggested that they talk to her separately and explain the consequences of her actions. Then, I asked them to hug her, as she was already very shocked by the incident.

Furthermore, I suggested that if they wanted to turn the mistake into a great educational moment, they should have unforgettable reactions. The parents thought about it and came up with an unusual gesture. They graciously showed their daughter that she was more valuable to them than all the money in the world by giving her twice as much money as she had stolen, even though it was a modest sum. They explained to her that honesty is the dignity of the strong ones.

She became thoughtful as a result of this approach. So, acceptance, understanding, and love were recorded in her memory, instead of being remembered as a thief and facing harsh punishment from her parents. The drama turned into a romance. The young girl never forgot how much her parents loved her and taught her throughout such a difficult moment. When she turned fifteen, she hugged her parents, saying that she had never forgotten that poetic moment. Everyone laughed. No scars remained.

A different case did not have the same outcome. A father was called to the police station because the security guard saw his son stealing a CD from a department store. The father felt humiliated. He was blind to the boy's anguish and the reality that his mistake was a perfect chance for him to demonstrate his maturity and wisdom. Instead, he slapped the son in front of the guards. When the boy got home, he locked himself in his room. When the father noticed his son was attempting suicide, he tried to break the door down. Feeling unworthy as a human being, the boy gave up on life in an impulsive act. The father never imagined he would lose his beloved son, and he was willing to sacrifice anything to bring him back.

Please, never punish someone when you are angry. As I have already mentioned, we are not giants, and we are capable of hurting the people we love the most during the first thirty seconds of anger. Do not let yourself be enslaved by your anger. When you feel that you are losing control, leave the scene, or you will react without thinking. Physical punishment should be avoided. Should some spank occur, it ought to be symbolic and followed by an explanation. Children and young people's intelligence will not be stimulated by the pain of spankings. The best way to assist them is by making them reevaluate their actions, examine themselves, and develop empathy.

You will be helping young people develop the following qualities in their personalities, by putting this instruction into practice: security in uncertain times, tolerance, leadership, and consideration. If a young person has hurt you, talk about your feelings with them. If necessary, cry with them. If your child has failed, discuss the causes of their failure, give them credit. The ability to reprimand someone with intelligence is a sign of maturity. For young people, we can be either executioners or heroes.

Never set limits without explanations. This is one of the most common capital sins that educators, whether parents or teachers, commit. In moments of anger, tense emotion blocks the memory fields. We lose rationality. So, stop! Wait for the temperature of your emotion to drop. If you really want to educate, use silence first, then ideas. The best punishment is one that is negotiated. Ask young people what they deserve for their mistakes. You will be surprised! They will reflect on their actions and may give themselves a more severe punishment than you would. Trust the intelligence of children and adolescents.

Penalties, restrictions, and other forms of punishment only serve to educate when they are not excessive and if they stimulate the art of thinking. Otherwise, it will be useless. Punishment is only useful when it is intelligent. Pain for the sake of pain is inhumane. Change your educational paradigms. Praise the youth before correcting or criticizing them. Tell them how important they are before pointing out their flaws. What will be the result? They will be more receptive to your observations and will love you forever.

5

Being impatient and giving up on educating

There was a very aggressive and agitated student who disturbed the class and frequently caused disruptions. He was insolent and disrespectful to everyone. He often repeated the same mistakes. He seemed incorrigible. Teachers could not stand him. They considered expelling him. However, before expelling him, a teacher stepped in and decided to invest in the student. Everyone thought it was a waste of time. Even without the support of his colleagues, he started talking to the boy during breaks. At first, it was a monologue, only the teacher spoke. Gradually, he began to engage the student, play with him, and take him out for ice cream. The teacher and the student built a bridge between their worlds. Have you ever built a bridge like this with difficult people?

The teacher found out that the boy's father was an alcoholic and abused both him and his mother. He realized that the seemingly insensitive boy had cried a lot, and now his tears had dried up. He understood that his aggression was a desperate reaction from someone who was asking for help. Yet no one understood his language. His screams were silent. It was so much easier to condemn him.

His mother's pain and his father's violence created conflict zones in the boy's memory. His aggression was an echo of the aggression he received. He was not a culprit; he was a victim. His emotional world had no colors. They denied him the freedom to smile, to play, and to face life with confidence.

Now, he was losing the right to study, to have the only chance to be a great man. He was about to be expelled.

When he realized what was taking place, the teacher started to win him over. The boy felt loved, supported, and valued. The teacher began to educate his emotions. During the first few days, he came to understand that behind every unruly student, behind every aggressive young person, there is a child in need of affection. It took only a few weeks for everyone to be amazed by his transformation. The rebellious boy began to be respectful. The aggressive boy began to be affectionate. He grew up to become an extraordinary adult. And all this happened because someone did not give up on him.

Everyone wants to educate sweet young people, but those who frustrate us are the ones that test the greatness of our love. Your complicated children are the ones testing your humanism. Fascinating teachers and brilliant parents never give up on their kids, even when they let them down and fail to show immediate improvement. Patience is their secret; the education of affection is their goal.

I would like you to believe that the young people who disappoint you the most today may be the ones who will bring you the most joy in the future. All you have to do is invest in them.

6

Failing to keep their word

There was a mother who could not say "no" to her son. She wanted to satisfy all of the boy's needs and demands since she could not stand his whining, tantrums, and general disruption. However, she could not always do so, and to avoid problems, she promised what she could not fulfill. She was afraid of disappointing her son. This mother was unaware that the process of developing personality requires frustration. Those who do not learn to deal with losses and frustrations will never mature. She kept her son from having momentary problems, but she was unaware that she was trapping him emotionally. What was the outcome?

This son lost respect for her. He began to manipulate her, exploit her, and engage in intense arguments with her. This story is because that son only valued the mother for what she had, not for who she was. As an adult, this boy experienced serious conflicts. Having spent his life witnessing his mother's deceit and unfulfilled promises, he projected a fatal distrust onto the social environment. He developed an insecure and paranoid emotion, believing that everyone wanted to deceive and betray him. He struggled to maintain jobs, establish enduring friendships, and develop ideas concerning persecution.

Social relationships are a signed contract on the stage of life. Do not break it. Do not disguise your reactions. Be honest with young people. Do not make this capital mistake. Keep your promises. If you cannot fulfill the request, do not be afraid to say "no", even if your child throws a tantrum. And if you make a mistake in this area, recognize it and apologize. Capital failures in education can be resolved when they are quickly corrected.

Trust is a skyscraper that is hard to build, easy to demolish, and extremely difficult to rebuild.

7

Destroying hope and dreams

The greatest capital sin that educators can commit is destroying hope and dreams of young people. Without hope, there is no road; without dreams, there is no motivation to walk ahead. Even if somebody has lost everything in life and the world may crumble on them, if they still have hope and dreams, they will have a sparkle in their eyes and joy in their soul.

There was a certain overly anxious father. He had a high academic background, and everyone respected him at the university. He often showed composure, eloquence, and insight in non-emotional decisions. However, when contradicted, he blocked his memory and reacted aggressively. This would mostly occur after he got home. In his department, he was sober, but at home, he was an unbearable man. He would have no patience with his children. He could not tolerate the slightest disappointment. Yet his negative reactions worsened when he found out that a son started doing drugs. Instead of embracing, helping, and encouraging him to overcome his struggles, he began to destroy the youth's hope. He said, "You will not amount to anything in life!" "You will become a criminal!"

The father's behavior further depressed the son and pushed him deeper into the dungeon of drugs. Unfortunately, the father did not stop there. In addition to destroying the son's hope, he obstructed his dreams, blocked his ability to find better days. He said, "You are hopeless," "You only bring me disgrace!" Some people who were close to this father thought that man had a split personality. However, from a scientific point of view, there is no split personality. Actually, two distinct memory reading fields are read in two different settings, leading to very distinct mental processes and emotional responses.

Many people are like lambs with other people, yet lions towards their family members. Why this paradox occurs? Because with other people they restrain themselves and do not open certain memory "slums", i.e., files that contain conflict zones. With the closest people, these ones lose the conscious brake and open the slums of the unconscious mind. This is the moment when anger, foolishness, and obsessive criticism emerge. In all people, this mechanism is present to a greater or lesser extent, even in the most sensible ones. We all tend to hurt the people we love the most. However, we cannot agree with that; otherwise, we risk destroying the dreams and hope of the people we care about the most.

Young people who lose hope struggle significantly to solve their conflicts. People who give up on their dreams become lifeless, uninteresting, and drawn to their own emotional miseries and defeats. Mental health requires believing in the most beautiful sunrise succeeding the stormiest night. The magnitude of our obstacles is not what matters; what matters is how driven we are to overcome them.

One of the greatest issues in psychiatry is not the severity of an illness, whether it is drug addiction, anxiety, phobia, depression, or drug addiction, but the Self's passivity. A passive, depressed Self, without hope or dreams, and resigned to its misfortunes, tend to carry its problems to the grave. An active, willing, bold Self can learn to manage thoughts, edit the film of the unconscious mind, and do things that exceed our imagination.

Psychiatrists, physicians, teachers, and parents are sellers of hope, merchants of dreams. A person only commits suicide when their dreams vanish, their hope dissipates. Without dreams, there is no emotional breath. Without hope, there is no nerve to live.

PART 4
The Five Roles of Human Memory

If time ages you physically, yet not emotionally,
you will always be happy.

Memory: The Secret Box of Personality

The memory is the ground where education grows. But has science unveiled what are the main roles of memory? It did, in part! Yet. many areas are still unknown. Millions of teachers around the world have been inadequately utilizing memory.

For instance, does recollection exist? Although many teachers and psychologists assure so, a pure recollection does not exist. Does memory storage depend on human will? Many scientists think so, but they are mistaken. Memory storage is automatic and involuntary. Can human memory be deleted like the computer's? Many users of these devices believe so, but it is impossible to delete human memory.

Memory is the secret box of personality. Everything we are, the world of thoughts, and the universe of emotions are produced from it. Our historical misrepresentations regarding memory seem like something out of fiction. For millennia we have been assigning functions to the memory that it does not have. In order to find the tools to rebuild education and revolutionize its concepts, we need to understand the five basic functions of the magnificent territory that is the memory. These functions have a role in the learning and knowledge construction. I will address the subject synthetically.

For those who wish to delve deeper into that, I suggest reading my book "Multifocal Intelligence" (Cury, 1998).

1

Memory registration is involuntary

Once, a man had a disagreement with a coworker. He felt he had been treated too unjustly. He told his coworker he would delete him from his life. Despite his tremendous effort to do so, the more he tried to forget his coworker, the more he thought about him, more reconstructing that feeling of injustice. Why could he not keep his promise? Because memory registration is automatic and it does not depend on human will.

Rejecting a negative idea can enslave us to it. If you reject someone, they might haunt your thoughts and keep you up at night. Forgiving them is emotionally more affordable. In computers, registration depends on a user command. In humans, registration is involuntary, performed by the AMR (Automatic Memory Recording) phenomenon. Every idea, thought, anxious reaction, moment of solitude, or period of insecurity is recorded in your memory and it becomes part of the mosaic of your existential history, the "movie" of your life.

Some implications of this role include:

- Taking care of our thoughts on the stage of our mind is taking care of our wellbeing;
- Taking care of what we feel in the present is taking care of our emotional future, of how happy, peaceful, and stable we will be;
- Personality is not static; its transformation depends on the quality of archiving experiences throughout life. Illness can strike at any point

in life, even in those who had a happy childhood. A cheerful child can become a sad adult; while a sad, traumatized child can become a happy, healthy adult;
- The quality of information and the registered experiences can turn the memory into a fertile ground or an arid desert, lacking creativity.

2

Emotion determines the quality of recording

A clinical psychologist asked a patient to recount details of his past. The patient struggled but could only talk about experiences that had marked him. He had lived millions of experiences, yet he could only discuss a few dozen.

The psychotherapist thought he was either blocked or suppressing. In fact, the patient was correct. We are only able to describe in full those events that include losses, joy, compliments, fear, and frustrations. Why is that so? Because the emotion determines the quality of the registration. The higher the emotional volume involved in an experience, the more privileged the registration will be, and the more chance it has of being retrieved. Where is it registered? In the MCU, which is the Memory of Continuous Usage, or conscious memory. Tense experiences are registered in the conscious center and will be continuously read from there. Over time, they are shifted to the unconscious periphery of the memory, called the EM, Existential Memory.

In certain instances, the level of anxiety or emotional stress might be so high that it results in a blockage in the memory. This blockage is an unconscious defense that prevents the retrieval and reproduction of emotional pain. This is the case of events involving traumas relating to war or accidents. Some children suffered so much in their childhood that they cannot recall that period of their lives. Frequently, experiences with a high emotional load remain available to be read and generate thousands of new thoughts and emotions. An unresolved conflict can ruin the day or a week. A feeling of rejection can imprison an entire life. A child trapped in a dark room can develop claustrophobia. Public embarrassment can generate social phobia.

Some implications of how the emotion interferes with the memory registration include:

- Teaching a subject by stimulating the students' emotions slows down thinking, improves concentration, and produces privileged registration;
- Teachers and parents who do not stimulate the emotions of young people do not educate; they only inform;
- Giving advice and guidance without emotion does not create "educational moments" in the memory trade;
- Small acts that evoke intense emotions have a greater impact on a child's personality development than yells and threats;
- Discriminatory jokes and derogatory nicknames carried on in the classroom can generate distressing experiences capable of producing serious conflicts;
- Protecting the emotion is essential for quality of life.

3

Memory cannot be deleted

In computers, the simplest task is to delete or erase any information. Yet this is not possible in human beings, with the exception of brain injuries. No matter how hard you try, you will not succeed in erasing your traumas, eliminating the people who have let you down, or forgetting the toughest moments in your life.

As we have seen, the only way to resolve our conflicts is to edit the memory files by registering new experiences over the negative ones in the archives where they are stored. As an example, security, peace, and joy should be filed upon the areas of the memory that contain experiences of insecurity and anxiety.

Numerous strategies, such as cognitive techniques that target symptoms or analytical techniques that address causes, can be used to edit the unconscious mind film. The combination of both is, ideally, the best option. A great way to combine them is by managing thoughts and emotions. In this way, we will become directors of the theater of our own minds instead of puppets of our inner conflicts.

Some implications of this role of memory include:

- Whether we want it or not, everything we think and feel will be recorded and will take part of the fabric of our story;

- Every single day, we can either plant flowers or accumulate trash in the soil of memory;
- Since deleting the past is impossible, reediting the film of the unconscious mind is the greatest possibility of incorporating new personality traits and overcoming traumas and emotional disorders;
- Editing the unconscious mind film or rewriting the memory is about building new experiences that will replace the old ones;
- The education that permeated the centuries was blind to the fact that we can become authors of our own story if we intelligently reedit the unconscious mind film. Otherwise, we will be victims of our miseries.

4

The degree to which memory windows open depends on emotion

The emotion not only determines whether a record will be fragile or privileged, but also determines the degree of openness of the files at a given moment. You have free access to the computer memory. In human intelligence, this access has to pass through the barrier of emotion. If a person is calm or anxious, the degree of openness of their memory, and consequently their ability to think, will be affected by these emotions.

Even though an executive may successfully prepare a presentation for the directors of the company, anxiety can cause him to stumble during the presentation. I have met many people whose hands are dry when they are alone but become cold and moist when greeting others. The excessive tension intellectually inhibits these people when they have to speak in public. The human memory is just not available when we want it. What determines the openness of the memory files is the emotional energy we experience at each given moment. Fear, anxiety, and stress lock the files and block thoughts.

Some implications derived from the relationship between emotion and the opening of memory include:

- Tranquility opens the memory windows and makes people more efficient in a contest or a work meeting;
- Anxiety can harm intellectual performance. Nervous tension can cause well-prepared students to perform poorly on a test;

- A tense or anxious person is ready to react instinctively, not to learn;
- To help or correct an anxious person, we must first conquer their emotion before conquering their reason.

5

Pure recollection does not exist

For thousands of years, we have built schools, believing in the existence of pure recollection. The fundamental principle of world education is "teach to remember and remember to apply". However, after many years of research on the roles of memory and the working of the mind, I am convinced that there is no pure recollection of the past, but rather the reconstruction of it with micro or macro differences.

I have already proven this. If you try to remember the thousands of thoughts you produced last week, you certainly will not recover the precise combination of verbs, pronouns, and nouns. Yet, if you recall the individuals and places you were in, it will help you recreate hundreds of new thoughts; though they will not be exactly what you originally thought. Likewise, if you try to remember the saddest or happiest day of your life, you will not retrieve the same thoughts and emotional reactions from that moment. Though not precisely the same, you may recreate similar emotions and thoughts. What does this demonstrate? That the memory is an expert at making us creators of new ideas. The past is a great foundation for building new experiences, not for living tied to it. Every time we live for the past, we block intelligence and become ill; this is also the case with losses and unresolved panic attacks. Fortunately, nothing is static in the psyche; everything can be overcome and reconstructed.

When you recall an experience with a childhood friend, a school game, or an emotional trauma, that recollection is never a pure recollection containing all the thoughts and emotional reactions you experienced at the time. It will always be a reconstruction, closer or further from the original experience. The reconstruction of the past is influenced by the "colors and flavors" of the present, such as the emotional state and social environment in which are. If we are at a party and recall an experience where we were rejected, we may only feel slight pain or even find it amusing. The social environment has become a variable that distorts the reconstruction.

Your memory is not an information repeating machine, like mere computers. It is a creation center. Set yourself free! Be creative! The following are some consequences and implications of the fact that there is no such thing as pure recollection:

- Multiple choice school exams do not measure the art of thinking. Sometimes, they nullify the reasoning of brilliant students;
- An excessive amount of information given in school is stressful;
- Most of the information is lost in the labyrinths of memory and will never be remembered again;
- The school model that privileges memory as a knowledge repository produces repeaters rather than thinkers;
- The fundamental goal of memory is to support creative, schematic, organizational thinking, and not for exact recollections.

PART 5

The School of Our Dreams – The school that raises thinkers in the 21st century: Revolutionizing Education

The better the quality of education, the less important will be the role of psychiatry in the third millennium.

The School of Life Project

The roles of memory, as well as the habits of brilliant and fascinating educators concisely presented here, will build up ten psychopedagogical tools or techniques that can be applied by parents and, especially, by teachers.

A large number of educators around the world affirm there is nothing innovative about education. Yet, I believe that something new and impactful will be presented here. These techniques contribute to changing education permanently. They constitute the School of Life project and can shape the education of our dreams. They can promote Piaget's constructivism dream, Vygotsky's art of thinking, Gardner's multiple intelligences, and Goleman's emotional intelligence.

The techniques will focus on improving the social and psychological environments of teachers and students rather than making adjustments to the adopted teaching materials or the physical surroundings. The application of these techniques in schools depends on human resources: teacher training and a change in the educational culture.

These techniques aim at educating the emotion, self-esteem, developing solidarity, tolerance, security, schematic reasoning, ability to manage thoughts under stressful situations, and how to cope with losses and disappointments. In short, they aim to shape thinkers.

1

Background music in the classroom

> *This technique aims to educate emotion, reduce anxiety,*
> *enhance concentration, develop a love for learning,*
> *and slow down thought processes.*

J.C. was born prematurely. Like many premature babies, he did not have the time to nestle into the uterine lap and take a month before facing the trials and tribulations of life. He was born seven months into pregnancy while he was still performing acrobatics inside his mother's womb. He was born full of energy. The surrounding stimuli disturbed him, leading to intense anxiety, and he became a hyperactive child. I have observed that a lot of premature newborns end up being hyperactive. Their hyperactivity is not genetic, but a result of the lack of emotional psychoadaptation, crucial at the final stage of gestation. Psychoadaptation occurs when the baby barely fits inside the womb, and, therefore, has to slow down its movements and learn to relax.

As a child, J.C. could not sit still in his chair. He was restless and tense; he repeated mistakes, and disrupted the class. Nothing calmed him down; even adult reprimands were ineffective. He was not like that because he wanted to. He had a vital need to disturb the environment to alleviate his anxiety. Concentration was a rare commodity. He only concentrated on what interested him a lot. The little concentration he had in class was enough to get good grades because he was actually a smart boy.

Over time, he learned how to manage his anxiety and have stable life projects. He had the help of teachers who applied some techniques I will later discuss. He became a competent worker. Like all hyperactive individuals, he had accelerated thinking. Now, guess what helped stabilize him? Classical music. Since childhood, his mother led him to appreciate it. Classical music slowed down his thoughts and stabilized his emotion. Examples like J.C.'s helped me understand the value of music in modulating the rhythm of thought. Here is the first psychopedagogical technique: background music during class presentations.

The Goals of Music in the Working of the Mind

If emotion affects the quality of recording, without emotion the transmission of information causes dispersion rather than focus and pleasure. Teachers of Math, Physics, Chemistry, or Language acquire an emotional dimension to their arid and rational knowledge when they have background music playing in the classroom, especially if it is soft music. The AMR phenomenon will register it in a privileged way. Without emotion, knowledge has no flavor.

Background music has three main goals: First, it provides musical and emotional education. Second, it generates the pleasure of learning during classes like Math, Physics, and History. Plato dreamt about the delights of learning. Third, it alleviates the Accelerated Thinking Syndrome (ATS) by calming the mind, improves concentration, and info assimilation. From an early age, background music should be played both at home and in the classroom.

The effects of background music in the classroom are spectacular. It relaxes teachers and cheers students. Young people love lively music because their thoughts and emotions are lively. However, after listening to calm music for six months, their emotions are trained and stabilized.

2

Seating in a circle or U-shape

> *This technique's goals are to develop security, promote participatory education, improve concentration, lessen classroom conflicts, and reduce classroom chatter.*

Once, when I was in the fifth grade of elementary school, my class was divided into groups. Every group had to present a project in front of the class. Many in my group refused to take on the task. Being braver, I went ahead. I had never trembled so much. My voice was muffled. It seemed so easy to speak in my room, but I could not organize my ideas in front of the class. Today, I give lectures to an audience of thousands of people. But it was not easy to overcome this conflict.

Why is it so hard to talk about our ideas in public? Why do many people struggle to raise their hand and ask questions in an auditorium? Why are some people eloquent and confident speaking with close friends but completely inhibited to discuss their opinions with strangers or in work groups? One of the main reasons is the school system.

Arranging students in a row behind one another in a classroom may seem innocuous, but it really hinders intelligence, causes distractions, and is harmful. Students' alignment kills spontaneity and destroys their confidence to express ideas. It creates a conflict characterized by fear and inhibition. The mechanism is as follows: when in a social environment, an unconscious phenomenon, called "memory trigger", is triggered in fractions of seconds. It opens certain files containing insecurity and blockages, generating stress that obstructs the reading of other files and hinders the ability to think.

Major educational theories did not study the roles of memory. Therefore, they did not realize that just two years of students sitting in rows in school are enough to generate an unconscious trauma. That is a trauma that causes great discomfort in expressing opinions in meetings, in saying "no", and addressing doubts in the classroom. Some people develop a dramatic fear of criticism and remain silent forever. Others are overly concerned about what others think and say about them. Do you have this trauma?

The traditional school system generates conflicts in students without realizing it. In addition to blocking the ability to argue, the alignment of students adds fuel to the accelerated thinking syndrome, ATS. The students' thinking goes a mile a minute. For adults, it's challenging enough to endure the fatigue, anxiety, and restlessness of ATS. Now, imagine children and young people forced to sit still, inert, and, moreover, having the back of their classmates' heads in front of them. They will disrupt the class, engage in side chats, and interact with their colleagues in an attempt to prevent exploding with anxiety. It's a matter of survival. Do not blame them. Blame the system.

How can this problem be solved? By having students sit in a semicircle, U-shape, or double circle. They need to see each other's faces. Kindly have students, from preschool to university, no longer sit in rows. It stimulates intellectual inertia.

Educating with the Eyes: Emotion Sculptors

Remember this phrase: the classroom is neither a silent army nor a stage with the teacher acting as the only performer and the students acting as passive spectators. Everyone is an actor in education. Education should be participatory. In my opinion, one-fifth of the school time should be spent with students giving lectures in front of the class. Teachers would relax during this period, and students would commit to education, develop critical thinking, schematic reasoning, and overcome social phobia.

I ask the teachers to pay special attention to shy students. They present varying degrees of social phobia, of sharing their opinions in public. We are creating a mass of shy young people. Shy people speak little but think a lot and sometimes their thoughts torment themselves. I have said it before – shy people are usually great for others but terrible for themselves. They are ethical and concerned about society, yet do not take care about their quality of life.

Educators are emotion sculptors. Educate by looking into the eyes, educate with gestures; they speak as much as words. Sitting in a U-shape or circle calms the mind, improves concentration, reduces students' anxiety. The class atmosphere becomes pleasant, and social interaction takes a significant leap.

3

Inquired presentation: The art of doubting

> *This strategy aims to: reduce ATS (Accelerated Thinking Syndrome), rekindle motivation, encourage questioning, improve text and statement interpretation, and open the windows of intelligence.*

Is all stress negative? No! Negative stress only occurs when it is intense, blocks intelligence, and causes symptoms. There is a type of positive stress that opens the windows of memory, stimulates us to overcome obstacles, and solves doubts. Without this stress, our dreams fade away and our motivation crumbles. Does education produce positive or negative stress? Often it produces negative one! Why? Due to the transmission of cold, conventional, and dull knowledge.

This transmission creates an atmosphere devoid of difficulties, excitement, and intellectual stimulation. Educating is provoking intelligence; it is the art of challenging. If teachers are unable to provoke the intelligence of their students during their presentation, they have failed to educate them. What is more important in education: doubts or answers? Many think it's the answer. But the answer is one of the greatest intellectual traps. The size of the answer is determined by the size of the doubt. Doubt instigates us much more than the answer.

Doubt is the beginning of wisdom in philosophy (Durant, 1996). A scientist, executive, or worker will excel and broaden their universe of ideas the more they doubt their own truths and question the world around them. Teachers ought to stimulate students' curiosity and provoke doubt among them. But how can they do that? By continuously conducting an inquired presentation. When talking about the atom, the teacher should ask: "Who can guarantee that the atom exists?", "How can we affirm that it is formed by protons, neutrons, and electrons?" Math, Language, and History teachers should learn to creatively question the knowledge they present. The words "Why?", "How?", "Where?", "What is the basis of this?" should be a part of their routine.

The inquired presentation generates doubt; doubt generates positive stress; and this stress opens the windows of intelligence. This is how we shape thinkers, not information repeaters. The inquired presentation first conquers the territory of the emotion, then the stage of logic, and finally, the soil of the memory. Students grow greatly driven, become questioners, instead of masses manipulated by the media and the system. The inquired presentation transforms information into knowledge, and knowledge into experience. The best teacher is not always the most eloquent but the one who stimulates intelligence the most.

Shaping Free Minds

If students spend four years in school only listening to information, they cease to be inquisitive about the world and themselves and turn into passive spectators. Some young people develop anxiety and psychopathy during this process, as well as becoming arrogant and insensitive.

What do psychopaths or dictators feed their intellect on? On absolute truths. They do not doubt, nor do they question their inhuman behaviors. The world revolves around their truths. They hurt others and do not feel their pain. Learning to embrace the art of doubt is essential for psychopaths to break free, since it allows them to reconsider and put themselves in other people's shoes.

Teachers must overcome the habit of transmitting conventional knowledge as if it were absolute truth. Additionally, a lot of "scientific facts" lose their significance and turn into folklore about every ten years. Practice making at least ten questions in each class. Do not think this is an easy task because it requires six months of training. Education emancipates and shapes free minds (Adorno, 1971), not mindless machines dictated by consumerism, aesthetic paranoia, and other's opinions.

4

Dialogical presentation: the art of asking questions

> *This technique's goals are to develop critical awareness, encourage intellectual discussion, encourage student participation in the classroom, overcome their shyness and insecurity, and improve concentration.*

A brilliant technique for transforming the lifeless classroom into a verdant garden is the dialogical presentation, which is carried out by the art of asking questions. In the inquired presentation, the teacher questions the students' knowledge without asking, while in the dialogical presentation, the teacher asks the students a great deal of questions, The two techniques complement each other. Let's see.

Through the art of asking questions, the teacher stimulates the positive stress of doubt even more. They captivate the students' attention and penetrate the territory of the emotion and the theater of their minds. Ready-made knowledge stops knowledge building, and doubt provokes intelligence (Vygotsky, 1987). All great thinkers were great askers of questions. Great answers came from great questions.

In what stage of life is it easier to learn? During childhood! Why is that so? Because this is the stage when we ask the most questions and open the windows of our minds. Children have an easier time learning languages because they interact more, ask questions, and have less information cluttered in their memory. Why does learning a foreign language become easier in its own country? The primary reason is that you feel embarrassed and face difficulties when you travel to another country. Diplomas and social standing are nearly worthless at this moment. In order to survive, you have to face embarrassment to establish a network of relationships. To accomplish this, you need to lose the fear of asking questions. This stressful situation facilitates learning by opening our memory archives in a remarkable way.

When a person stops asking, they stop learning and stop growing. When do scientists produce their brightest ideas? When they are mature or when they are still immature? When immature, because they doubt, stress, and ask more. Einstein proposed the theory of relativity at 27. After scientists are bestowed with titles and honors, problems surface. The same honors and recognition that bring them acclaim can also act as a poison, destroying their ability to think (Cury, 2002). Many of them become sterile.

My books are currently being published in more than forty countries. As a researcher of the backstage of the mind, I am concerned because even if I do not want to, I know that this success has already caused some damage to my unconscious mind. To be an engineer of new ideas, I have to be alert, continuously empty and recycle myself. Do you still have a committed appetite for learning, or have you stopped? Many do not realize that they have stopped thinking...

During class, a fascinating teacher must bring up at least ten questions to the students. They should first ask the question to the whole class. The question will positively stress the students and improve concentration. If no one dares to answer, the teacher should call a student by name and ask them. Regardless of the answer, the student should be praised for their participation. Shy students are won over by this procedure.

Traveling within themselves

The art of asking questions generates brilliant thinkers in Medicine, Law, Engineering, Pedagogy, and so on. But it must start in preschool. After a year using the art of inquired and dialogical presentations, students lose their fear of expressing themselves, learn to discuss ideas, and become great travelers. How come? They learn how to travel within themselves, learn to ask questions why they are distressed, anxious, irritated, lonely, or frightened. They learn not only to question the outside world but also to have a roundtable discussion with themselves.

When I train psychologists for clinical practice, I always talk to them about the greatness of this inner roundtable discussion. Whoever is capable of conducting this self-dialogue edits the unconscious mind film more quickly and efficiently. It is not enough for a patient to undergo psychotherapy. They must be the author of their story, learn to intervene in their own world. But regrettably, even in the medical field, people hardly ever penetrate their own world. Loneliness is manageable when the world abandons us, but it is quite unbearable when we give up on ourselves.

The art of asking questions is part of the education of our dreams. It transforms the classroom and our emotional room into a poetic, pleasant and intelligent space.

5

Being a storyteller

> *The purposes of this technique are to enhance socializing, stimulate creativity, educate the emotion, increase knowledge, and enhance one's ability to solve problems under pressure.*

Education is storytelling. Telling stories is turning life into society's most serious recreation. Life has losses and problems, but it should be lived with optimism, hope, and joy. Parents and teachers should dance the waltz of life as storytellers. The world is too serious and cold. Daily news reports crimes, disasters, deaths, and misfortunes. The memory stores all of this flood of negative information, which creates chains of thoughts that make life depressing, anxious, and unenthusiastic.

We need to live gentler, learn to laugh at our silliness, absurd behaviors, quirks, and fears. We need to tell more stories. Parents need to teach their children by creating stories. Teachers need to tell stories to teach classes with the spice of joy and, at times, tears. It takes a fluctuating, theatricalized voice that shifts into a different tone during a storytelling presentation. It's essential to produce gestures and reactions capable of expressing what logical information cannot. Despite having excellent academic cultures, many parents and teachers are stiff, formal, and rigid. Not even they can stand themselves.

Are there people who cannot tell stories? I do not believe so. Inside every human being, even the most formal ones, there is a "clown" who wants to breathe, play, and relax. Let it live. Surprise the youth. Our children need a serious education, but it must also be pleasant. Smile, embrace the youth, tell them stories.

Shouting inside the heart; telling gentle stories

"Stories" may rescue "history". Fiction can rescue reality. How can it be? For example, Black enslavement should never be discussed by a history teacher without first preserving the relevant historical context. Dry information regarding slavery do not elicit sensitization, education, consciousness, and repudiation of the crimes our species has committed.

When talking about Black people, History teachers should provide narratives that help students understand the hopelessness, agony, and despair experienced by these people who were being enslaved by their own kind. Nothing better than telling a real story or creating a "story" to make students experience the drama of slavery.

Without this inner reflection, slavery does not generate a solid emotional impact; it does not spark a forceful uprising against prejudice; the death of millions of Jews, Romani people, and other minorities does not generate commotion, nor does it create intellectual vaccines. This way, other "Hitlers" will arise. Speaking about knowledge without humanizing it and without rescuing the emotion of the history behind it, is something that just perpetuates our miseries and does not cure them.

Telling stories is also psychotherapeutic. What is the most effective method for resolving conflicts in the classroom? It is not to lecture, yell, or act aggressively. These methods have been used since the Stone Age and have never worked. But telling stories do. Telling stories hooks the thought, it stimulates critical thinking. The next time a student or a child attacks you, make them think. Politely shout inside them, shout gently, tell them a story. Your rules and criticisms may be forgotten by young people, but the stories you tell will stay with them forever.

6
Humanizing knowledge

> *This technique aims to: stimulate boldness, develop insight and creativity, encourage wisdom, develop critical thinking skills, and shape thinkers.*

Classic education system makes another big mistake: It makes an effort to impart knowledge in the classroom, yet it rarely comments on the life of the one who produced that knowledge. Information about Chemistry, Physics, Mathematics, Languages should have a face, an identity. It all should make a sense!

It means humanizing knowledge, telling the story of the scientists who produced the ideas that the teachers are addressing. It also means reconstructing the emotional weather they lived in while researching. It also means reporting the anxiety, mistakes, difficulties, and discriminations they suffered. Some thinkers died defending their ideas! The best way to raise people who do not think is to feed them lifeless, depersonalized knowledge. I am critical about well-designed educational resources that expose knowledge without considering the story of the scientists. Students that receive this kind of education develop aversion rather than the ability to think critically.

How many restless nights, challenges, and troubles have I gone through to come up with a new theory regarding the working of the mind in a nation that has no tradition of creating theoretical scientists! It takes more work to produce a new theory than to complete hundreds of research projects. But not everyone values this work.

What are my intellectual pillars? Will it be my accomplishments, the theory's acceptance, and its application in theses for master's and doctoral degrees? No! My pillars are the suffering I endured, the uncertainties I experienced, the anxieties I had, and the overcoming of my chaos.

Behind every piece of information given in the classroom there are the tears, adventures and courage of the scientists; but the students cannot see them. That's why talking about the story of science and the story of the thinkers is as important as talking about the knowledge they have produced. Science without a face paralyzes intelligence, decharacterizes being, brings it closer to nothing (Sartre, 1997). It generates arrogant men, not men who think. Rarely has a scientist caused harm to humanity. Those who caused harm were those who used science without critical consciousness.

Passion for science: in search of adventurers

Since I produce knowledge about how we construct thoughts, it has always intrigued me to see that in the first generation, a thinker creates a group of fellow thinkers, and in the second generation they become scarce. For instance, several of Freud's early friends, including Jung and Adler, went on to become thinkers. After Freud's death, many of his followers closed themselves to new possibilities of thinking. As a result, they merely replicated or copied the ideas of the first generation rather than expanding upon them.

Why does this unconscious phenomenon occur in science? Because the first generation took part in the living history of that thinker. They opened the windows of their intelligence and ventured to invent, take chances, and suggest something new because they felt the warmth of his challenges, persecutions, and courage. The second generation did not participate in this history, so they have deified, rather than humanized the thinker.

Of course, there are exceptions, but this mechanism is universal. It has always been present in Philosophy, Law, Physics, the political system, and even among spiritual leaders. Do you know what are the worst enemies of a theory and an ideology? It's their radical defenders. Though there is much to discuss about this topic, now it's not the time for that.

In light of this, I firmly contend that revolutionizing education requires humanizing knowledge. Otherwise, we will attend thousands of education congresses that will have no intellectual effect. Even with master's and doctoral degrees, students will only play a supporting role in the advancement of science. I believe that teachers should spend 10 to 20% of the time of every class rescuing the story of the scientists who produced that knowledge. This technique stimulates passion for knowledge and produces engineers of ideas. Students will depart with a diploma in hand and passion in their hearts. They will be adventurous individuals who will successfully face and explore the world.

After high school and college, young people will want to take after successful entrepreneurs such as scientists, physicians, lawyers, teachers; in short, people who change the world, rather than overnight celebrities and photogenic models. The faceless knowledge and the unrealistic entertainment industry are destroying our real heroes.

7

Humanizing the teacher: crossing their story

> *The goals of this method are to encourage socialization, stimulate affection, build a productive social bridge, encourage wisdom, resolve conflicts, and value the "being".*

Before the 16th century, education was usually carried out by teachers who lived with the young people. During their teenage years, these youth would move away from their parents and learn professions in blacksmithing, winemaking, etc. Many of them paid a huge emotional price as a result of their separation from their parents from the ages of 7 and 14, which weakened their emotional bond with them.

When schools became more widespread, there was a significant emotional leap. Apart from the educational progress they made in schools, children returned home every day to spend time with their parents. Affection between them grew. Parents hugged their children every day. Words like "cher" (dear) appeared in France. Even the architecture of houses changed. Lateral corridors were introduced to prevent strangers from invading the family's intimate space.

As soon as schools became widespread, they injected fuel into social relationships. It was a beautiful beginning. The family was a feast. Parents had time for their children, and the children admired their parents. However, these links would become increasingly distant over the following centuries. Today, parents and children barely have time to talk. And what about the school relationship? It's even worse! Teachers and students share the same classroom space, yet they do not know each other. Despite spending years together, they still remain strangers to one another. What kind of education ignores the emotion and denies existential story?

Animals do not have a life story because they do not perceive themselves as distinct from the world. However, human beings recognize this difference and, therefore, construct a story and transform the world (Freire, 1998). Pedagogy schools fail by not encouraging their teachers to humanize themselves in the classroom. It is essential to humanize knowledge and, more importantly, to humanize the teachers. Students can get information from computers, yet only teachers have the power to shape it. They alone possess the ability to stimulate creativity, resolving of conflicts, joy with existence, education for peace, for consumption, and the defense of human rights.

Teachers, each one of you has an amazing story full of happiness and sorrows, dreams and frustrations. Little by little, share your story with your students throughout the year. Do not hide behind the chalk or your subject. Otherwise, transversal themes – responsible for imparting life lessons, including those related to consumption, traffic, health, and peace – will be a utopia, existing in the legislation but not in the heart.

Modern education is in crisis because it is not humanized; it separates the thinker from knowledge, the teacher from the subject, the student from the school, ultimately separating the subject from the object. It has developed rational youth who are proficient with math and technology yet find it difficult to overcome obstacles, conflicts, contradictions, and challenges. As a result, it rarely yields exceptional professionals and executives – individuals who truly excel and make a difference.

Low grades hold great value in the school of life

Dear teachers, set aside some time during class to discuss your challenges, aspirations, failures, and accomplishments. What will be the result? You will educate the emotions. Your students will love you, and you will become unforgettable teachers. They will appreciate your classes and relate to the subject you teach. Make sure to listen to your students. Enter their world. Find out who they are. Students' personalities are shaped more by their educators' being than by their teachers' knowledge.

Dear parents, you also have a brilliant story. As I mentioned at the beginning of this book, talk about yourselves, let your children find out your world. Sharing your dreams, successes, insecurities, and failures is the best way to prepare them for life, rather than imposing rules, criticizing, scolding, or punishing them.

Fascinating educators are not perfect. On the contrary, they take responsibility for their mistakes, they are willing to reconsider their positions when convinced, and refrain from imposing their beliefs on their children and students. The AMR phenomenon (Automatic Memory Recording) records these lucid behaviors in a remarkable way, creating a garden in the conscious and unconscious world of their young minds.

Consider this example: Jesus Christ did not control anyone; He simply presented His ideas and invited people to reflect, saying: "whoever is thirsty...", "whoever wants to follow me...". He encouraged the art of thinking. The great peacemakers, such as Plato, Buddha, Mohammed, Gandhi, aimed to shape free men. In the school of life, low grades help us more than high grades. In certain cases, failing can lead to a richer experience than succeeding. We need to talk about our victories, but also about our frustrations. Many young people who are depressed and phobic are pleading with their gesturing and attitudes for a teacher to tell them a story that can help in some way.

Once, a pedagogical coordinator from a large school, who happened to be at one of my conferences, inspired by the presentation, stood up in front of the crowd and shared a touching story. She mentioned that a student approached her a few months earlier to talk about a problem. She had told the student she didn't have time at that moment for the conversation and postponed it to another day, even though the student was visibly distressed. Sadly, there was not enough time because the young girl took her own life prior to their scheduled meeting. A few minutes had never been so crucial.

How many conflicts could have been avoided through a humanized education!? I have no doubt that teachers who read this book and start interacting with their aggressive, anxious or repressed students will prevent a great deal of suicides as well as shooting sprees in which teenagers pull out guns and shoot classmates and teachers.

Young people screamed for help in numerous ways before committing these atrocities, but no one heard them. They cried out, but no one understood their message. A lot of people have told me that they gave up on the idea of committing suicide based on the dialogue I had with them. When we listen to these people, they also listen to themselves and find their paths. But there are many who are afraid to listen.

Remember that conflict prevention is not solely the responsibility of psychologists and psychiatrists. After all, it is the minority that seeks psychological help. Teachers can do much more than they imagine.

Gaining competitive advantages

Let me insist on this point, as it can never be emphasized enough. Unfortunately, the education around the world is wrong. Schools were born without a profound understanding of the roles of the memory and the thought building process. Even in the absence of statistical data, as I have mentioned earlier, I believe at least 90% of the knowledge we receive in the classroom will be forgotten.

We overwhelm the memory, not knowing what to do with too much information. The memory specializes in sustaining the blossoming of new thoughts, the creativity of intelligence. Let's provide less information and intertwine more of our stories. Most schools only focus on preparing students for acceptance into prestigious colleges. Their mistake is focusing solely on this goal. Even if these students get into the best universities, they may have a very hard time addressing their personal and professional challenges after finishing college.

The educational system is ill. Go beyond the program content. I ask for teachers to find spaces to humanize knowledge, humanize your story, and stimulate the art of doubt. In addition to intellectual growth, your students will also have competitive advantages. What advantages?

They will be entrepreneurs, will know how to make choices, take risks to achieve their goals, endure the winters of life with dignity. They will be emotionally healthier, less likely to develop conflicts, and less likely to need psychological treatment.

8

Educating the self-esteem: praising before criticizing

> *This method aims to educate the emotion and self-esteem, vaccinate against discrimination, promote solidarity, resolve classroom conflicts, filter stressful stimuli, and deal with frustrations and losses.*

Praise soothes the wounds of the soul, educates the emotions and self-esteem. Praising is encouraging and highlighting positive characteristics. There are parents and teachers who never praise their children and students.

The book by my authorship "You are Irreplaceable" became a significant editorial sensation in many countries, not because I am a great writer, but because I praise life in it. I wrote that we all commit crazy acts of love in order to be alive. We were the greatest mountain climbers and the greatest swimmers in the world to win the greatest race in history, a race with more than 40 million contenders. Do you know what race I am talking about?

The spermatozoon's race to fertilize the egg. It was a great adventure. Many young people say they didn't ask to be born. Others get discouraged when facing problems. Others, nevertheless, believe that nothing in their life is going well. But we are all born winners. All current difficulties we confront pale in comparison to the serious risks we took in order to survive on the stage of existence. Teachers need to communicate this story to students. It has contributed to building a solid self-esteem.

How to help a student or a child who failed, behaved aggressively, or had unacceptable reactions? Use the praise-criticize technique. First, praise some of their characteristics. Praise stimulates pleasure and pleasure opens the memory windows. Moments later, you can criticize and lead them to reflect on their failure. Criticizing first without praising obstructs intelligence, leading the young person to react instinctively, like a threatened animal. Even the most aggressive person becomes vulnerable and receptive to assistance when they receive praise. Many murders could be avoided if, in the first minute of tension, the threatened person praised their aggressor.

A man of German descent, whose grandparents had experienced the horrors of war, once visited my office. He was very aggressive. He claimed he would kill anyone who crossed his path, including his children. I mentioned something in a session that he didn't like and he threatened me by pulling out a concealed weapon. What do you think I did next? I stood my ground. I looked him in the eyes and praised him. I said, "How can such an intelligent man need a weapon to express his ideas?" And I continued, "You know you have great intellectual capacity and you can conquer anyone through it."

The praise surprised him. His anger melted like ice in the hot sun. He started crying. From that moment on, he had an excellent progress in his treatment. He became a kind human being. Had I not taken that approach, I might not be here today to share this story.

Vaccinating against discrimination

Try complimenting your spouse, children, coworkers, and students before you criticize them. There are always reasons to value someone; find them. After praising them, provide your criticism, yet say it just once. The repetition of critical words is not what provides the educational moment, but their privileged record does. After applying this technique for a few months, your relationships with others will completely change. You will be able to win over even the most unbearable and coldest people.

There are not "problematic young people", only young people who are going through problems. Compliment shy, obese, victimized, hyperactive, difficult and aggressive young people. Encourage those who have suffered from mocking, who feel inferior. Being an educator is being a promoter of self-esteem. If I could, I would visit schools all around the world to train teachers to understand the workings of the mind and to realize that even in small classroom settings, profound emotional traumas can occur. People express criticism much more than praise. Often, students seriously hurt each other.

Students should never be allowed to refer to their obese classmates as "whale" or "elephant" because of this. You cannot imagine the emotional damage that these nicknames cause in the soil of the unconscious mind. Never allow them to speak derogatorily about others' physical disabilities or skin color. These are not innocent jokes. They generate serious conflicts that do not fade away; it is something that will always reappear. Discrimination is a cancer, a blemish that has always tainted human history.

From an early age, I taught my daughters to understand that behind every human being, there is a world to be discovered. They have learned how to deal with discrimination. I am of European and Asian descent. Guess what color were the dolls of my two youngest daughters, by their ages nine and ten: Black. Even though we are white, they went to sleep happily with their black dolls. I did not intervene in their choice. They have learned to love life.

Teach young people to love the human species through your words and, most importantly, through your attitudes. Observe that aside from the fact that we are Americans, Arabs, Jews, whites, blacks, rich, and poor, we are a fascinating species. In the backstage of our intelligence, we are just equal – more than we can imagine. Praise life. Lead young people to dream. There will be no future if they stop believing in life.

9

Managing thoughts and emotions

> *The goals of this method are: to restore self-leadership, resolve ATS, prevent conflicts, protect the memory soils, promote security, develop an entrepreneurial mindset, and shield the emotions during stressful situations.*

I was once approached by an engineering student complaining about depression. She had seen seven psychiatrists and taken nearly every kind of medication available for depression. She was discouraged. Life had no color for her. Hope had dissipated. The final stage of human suffering, the pain of depression, had robbed her of her life's purpose. I was moved by her emotional distress. I told her not to settle with just being a patient; That she could turn the game around.

By regaining control over her Self, she could enhance the effects of the medications and bring back her sense of joy with life. I stated that she possessed unused tools inside herself. I mentioned that, despite its importance, medication played a supporting role in the treatment. Who is the main actor? It is the management of negative thoughts and of distressing emotions. She learned that all the garbage going through the stage of her mind was automatically registered in her memory and could no longer be deleted, only reedited. She realized that she should not only understand the miseries of her past in order to make this reediting occur, but also criticize every negative thought and disturbing emotion.

And so, little by little, the frail young woman ceased to be the victim of her problems and started to write a new chapter in her life and contemplate the beauty. Flowers blossomed after the long and harsh winter. She became more beautiful. All people who go through the chaos of depression, panic, phobias, losses, and overcome them become more beautiful inside.

Self-pity, conformity, and lack of determination to fight are serious obstacles to overcoming emotional disorders. Thought management is the central point of psychotherapeutic treatment of any theoretical current. Nevertheless, despite science's limited understanding of this topic, we also need to understand that this management is the central point of education. If young people do not learn how to manage their thoughts, they will be like a boat without a rudder; they will become like puppets of their own problems. The primary goal of education is to make a person a leader of oneself, a leader of one's thoughts and emotions.

All around the world, schools prepare students for managing businesses and machinery, but not to direct the script of their thoughts. There are countless people who are professionally successful but slaves to their thoughts. Their emotional life is miserable. They can face the world, but they cannot clear their minds from all the garbage.

I have treated intelligent people who can solve objective problems, such as doctors, lawyers, and entrepreneurs. On the other hand, they are defeated by an offense, destroyed by criticism, and a disappointment on the part of their loved ones causes great anxiety. In the outside world, they exhibit strength, but within the ground of their psyche, they are fragile leaders.

Freeing oneself from intellectual imprisonment

Fascinating teachers must help their students free themselves from intellectual imprisonment. How can they do that? Regardless of the subject they teach, they must show, at least once a week, that the students can and should manage their thoughts and emotions.

Whether by telling stories or speaking directly, teachers should emphasize that if the conscious will, representing the Self, does not lead one's thoughts, they will be dominated. There cannot be two masters. They should mention that human beings tend to be their own executioners. The teachers need to emphasize that our worst enemies are within us. We are the only ones who can stop ourselves from being happy and healthy.

In the same way, parents need to teach their children to criticize their own negative ideas, to turn the table on their fears, to face their sorrows and shyness. One of the most significant scientific breakthroughs of our day, in my opinion, is the thought management, which has broad applications in psychology and education. However, education, pedagogy schools, and psychology colleges still fall behind in this area. We are experts in growing passive people.

What is the point of learning to solve math problems if our young people do not learn how to solve life problems? What is the point of learning languages if they do not know how to speak about themselves? It is time to generate authors rather than those who are victims of their own history. It is time to prevent emotional illnesses among young people, rather than treating them after they emerge. Young people need an extraordinary education.

10

Engaging in social projects

> *This technique's goals are to: develop social responsibility, promote a sense of social duty, encourage solidarity, increase teamwork skills, and focus on cross-cutting issues such as education for human rights, health, and peace.*

The tenth pedagogical technique that I propose is leading young people to engage in social projects. Social commitment ought to be education's main objective. In its absence, selfishness, individualism, and the dominance of some over others will thrive. Engaging in initiatives aimed at preventing drug abuse, violence, AIDS, and famine can help develop young people's social and emotional health. They enjoy the poison of immediate pleasure and consumerism, as we have seen. Most of them only care about themselves. Yet, I reiterate, they are not to blame. Without them even realizing it, there are millions of images recorded in their conscious and unconscious memory that control them.

In reality, we are all victims of the system we create. We are increasingly losing our identity, turning into nothing but a bank account, a credit card number, or a potential consumer. My criticism is well-founded: The social system infiltrates the secrets box of the personality, dwindling the production of simple, tranquil, and serene thoughts.

The results of a survey that I carried out with approximately one thousand educators addressing their perceptions of young people's quality of life were astonishing. According to them, 94% of youth are aggressive, 6% are tranquil, 95% are alienated, and 4% have concerns about their future. What future lies for education?

Young people who make a difference

Determined, creative, and entrepreneurial young people will survive in the competitive system, while people who lack ambition and the courage to materialize their projects may find themselves in their parents' shadows and contributing to the unemployment rate. Intellectually unqualified young people harm the future of a nation. Why does a country's wealth fluctuate? Why do not family fortunes last until the third generation? Because of human matter.

We need to educate our children and students. They must feel important in school, they need to be trained to become leaders. They should be involved in decisions that affect the entire family, including financial planning, traveling, dining out, and buying a car. They need to learn how to make choices. With this, they will learn a hard lesson: choices also imply losses and not only gains.

The ATS syndrome causes our children to be restless. They hate routine, and therefore, they complain that "they have nothing to do". In fact, they have a lot to do, but routine intensifies anxiety. If we engage them in social projects, their lives will take a turn. They will have their emotion structured, their thoughts calmed, and in addition, they will learn the importance of serving others. How can they climb the podium if they despise training? How will they excel in society if they have no connection with it? It is an insult to our children's and students' intelligence if we see them only as information receivers and consumers of material goods.

We need to train young people who make a difference in the world, who propose changes, who rescue their existential sense and the meaning of things (Ricoeur, 1960). One of the causes that lead millions of young people to drug abuse, suffer depression, become alienated, and even consider committing suicide is that they have no meaning in life, or social engagement. Boredom consumes them. As a result, in an insane attitude, they turn to drug abuse as an attempt to alleviate their anxiety and distress, not just to satisfy their curiosity. Many young people use drugs like antidepressants and tranquilizers. Unfortunately, this attitude leads them to live in the most dramatic prison of all: the emotional prison.

Education needs a revolution, not merely a reform. The education of the future needs to shape thinkers, entrepreneurs, dreamers, leaders not only of the world we live in, but also for the world we are.

Applying the techniques of the School of Life Project

We must not forget that teachers around the world are collectively becoming ill. Teachers are chefs of knowledge, but they cook for a group of people who are not hungry. Every mother gets a bit paranoid when her children do not eat. How can we demand that teachers be healthy if their students have intellectual anorexia? It is for the sake of their health and that of their students that education needs to be rebuilt.

Schools that have already employed the ten pedagogical techniques of the School of Life project are experiencing something amazing. Teachers' stress levels have dropped, as have the pleas for silence in the classroom. Anxiety levels, simultaneous conversations, and conflicts have decreased. There has been an improvement in participation, concentration, and appreciation of the learning process.

After reading my books, the principal of a public school asked my help. She had to frequently call the police in order to contain aggression among students. Moved, I trained the teachers. They applied all these techniques for a year. What was the result? In addition to all the intellectual gains I had mentioned earlier, the police were no longer necessary. There were no more shouting, the students calmed down, and respect emerged. This public school only offered elementary education. When the students entered another school for high school, the teachers were impressed with their tranquility. They became poets of life.

Faced with such significant changes, the principal told me, "I cannot believe what happened to my school!" I did not do much; the teachers deserve all the praise. This may be one of the rare cases in the world where the use of psychopedagogical techniques has resulted in significant changes in personality dynamics and in the educational process. The best part is that using these techniques does not require money. It generates the school of our dreams. I hope thousands of schools around the world join this dream.

What is the school of your dreams? For me, it is the school that educates young people to draw strength from weakness, security from the shadow of fear, hope from desolation, a smile from tears, and wisdom from failures. The school of my dreams combines the seriousness of an executive with the happiness of a clown, the strength of logic with the simplicity of love. In the school of my dreams, every child is a unique jewel in the theater of existence, valued more than all the money in the world. In it, teachers and students write a beautiful story, they are gardeners who turn the classroom into a flowerbed of thinkers.

What is the family of your dreams? The family of my dreams is not perfect. It does not have perfect parents or children who never cause frustrations. It is one in which parents and children have the courage to say to each other: "I love you," "I overreacted," "I'm sorry," "You are important to me." In the family of my dreams, there are no heroes or giants, but friends. Friends who dream, love, and cry together. In it, children make fun of their own stubbornness, and parents laugh when they become impatient. The family of my dreams is a feast. It is somewhere simple, a place where people are happy.

PART 6
The Great Tower Story

> *If half of the budget destinated to worldwide military spending was used for educational purposes, generals would become gardeners, police officers would become poets, psychiatrists would become musicians. Violence, hunger, fear, terrorism, and emotional problems would only be found in the pages of dictionaries, not in the pages of life...*

Who are the most important workers in society?

I will share a story[1] that highlights the perilous path society is taking, the educational crisis, and the critical role that parents and educators have in shaping a better world. I have told this story in many conferences, including international congresses. Many educators are deeply touched to the extent that they end up shedding tears:

In a not-too-distant period from our own, humanity became so chaotic that people organized a major competition. They wanted to know which profession was the most important to society. Inside a massive stadium, the event planners built a tall tower with golden steps adorned with precious stones. The tower was beautiful. They invited the world press, TV, newspapers, magazines, and radio to cover the event.

The world was tuned in to the event. People from every social class crowded to the stadium to watch the competition up close. The rules were as follows: each profession was represented by a distinguished speaker. The speaker had to quickly climb a step of the tower and deliver an eloquent and convincing speech about why their profession was the most important to modern society. The speaker had to remain on the tower until the end of the competition. Voting took place online and was open to all users worldwide. Nations and large companies sponsored the competition. Government subsidies, a substantial amount of money, and societal status would all be

---

[1] Both the publisher and the author allow the use of the "Great Tower" text for theatrical performances in schools, with the aim of honoring parents and teachers, as long as the source is cited.

awarded to the winning category. The competition started once the rules had been established. The contest mediator exclaimed, "Let the competition begin!"

Do you know who climbed the tower first? Educators? No! It was the psychiatrist, who represents my profession. He climbed the tower and loudly proclaimed, "Modern societies will become stress factories. Depression and anxiety are the illnesses of the century. People have lost the allure of existence. Many give up on life. The industry of antidepressants and tranquilizers has become the most important in the world." Then, the speaker paused. The amazed audience listened attentively to his compelling arguments.

The representative of psychiatrists concluded, "Conflicts are normal, and being healthy is abnormal. What would humanity be without psychiatrists? Nothing but an institution for humans with no quality of life! Because we live in a society that is ill, I declare that we, along with clinical psychologists, are the most important professionals in society!"

Silence took over the stadium. Many in the audience looked at themselves and realized they were not happy; they were stressed, slept poorly, woke up tired, had a restless mind, and headaches. Millions of spectators were speechless. The psychiatrists seemed unbeatable. The mediator then exclaimed, "Who is the next contender?!" Do you know who climbed next? Teachers? No! It was the representative of the judiciary – the judge.

He climbed a higher step and spoke boldly, shocking the listeners: "Look at the violence rates! They keep increasing. Kidnappings, robberies, and traffic violence fill the pages of the newspapers. Aggression in schools, child abuse, racial and social discrimination are part of our routine. Men love their rights and despise their duties."

The listeners nodded in agreement with the presented arguments. Then, the representative of the judiciary was more compelling: "Drug trafficking moves as much money as oil. Organized crime cannot be eradicated. If you want security, imprison yourselves at home because freedom belongs to criminals. Without judges and prosecutors, society falls apart. Therefore, I declare, with the support of the prosecutors and the police force, that we represent the most important class in society." These words were hard to swallow. They were hard to listen to and burned in the soul. Yet they seemed undeniable. It took another moment of silence, this one lasting longer. Then, the sweating mediator said: "Who wants to come up next?!"

Another audacious representative climbed a higher step of the tower. Do you know who it was this time? Educators? Not yet! It was the representative of the armed forces. With a vibrant voice and no delay, he spoke: "Men disregard the value of life. They kill each other for very little. Terrorism eliminates thousands of people. Trade war causes millions to starve. The human species has been divided into dozens of tribes. Nations only respect each other based on the economy and the weapons they possess. If you want peace, prepare for war. The balancing elements in a corrupt world are not discourse but rather economic and military strength."

His words shocked the listeners, but they were unquestionable. He then concluded: "Without the armed forces, there would be no security. Sleep would be a nightmare. Therefore, I declare, whether you accept or not, that the men of the armed forces are not only the most important professional class but also the most powerful." The listeners' soul froze. Everyone was stunned. The arguments of the three speakers were very strong. Society had become chaos. People around the world were confused and unsure of what to do: whether to applaud the speaker or to mourn the crisis of the human species, which did not honor its ability to think.

No one dared to climb the tower anymore. Who would they cast their votes for? Just as everyone assumed the competition was over, there was a discussion at the base of the tower. Who were they? This time, it was the teachers. There was a group of them from preschool, elementary, high school, and university. They leaned against the tower, dialoguing with a group of parents. No one knew what they were doing. The TV focused on them and projected them on a big screen. The mediator shouted for one of them to climb the tower. They refused.

The mediator teased them: "There are always cowards in a competition." Laughter echoed in the stadium. They ridiculed both teachers and parents. The crowed viewed then as weak, but the teachers, being encouraged by the parents, began to debate ideas, staying in the same place. All of them were represented. One of the teachers, looking up, said to the representative of the psychiatrists: "We do not want to be more important than you. All we want is an environment to educate the emotions of our students, to form free and happy young people so they will not get ill and require your care." The psychiatrists' representative felt like an arrow had pierced his soul.

Then, another teacher on the right side of the tower looked at the representative of the judges and said: "We never aimed at being more important than judges. All we want is to be able to shape our youth's intelligence, making them love the art of thinking and learn the greatness of human rights and duties. Thus, we hope they never find themselves in the defendant's seat." The representative of the judiciary trembled on the tower.

A teacher on the left side of the tower, apparently shy, faced the representative of the armed forces and spoke poetically: "Teachers around the world never wanted to be more powerful or more important than members of the armed forces. We just want to be important in the hearts of our children. We aim to help them understand that every human being is not just another number in the crowd but an irreplaceable being, a unique actor in the theater of existence."

The teacher paused and added: "As a consequence, they will fall in love with life, and when they are in control of society, they will never wage wars, whether physical ones that spill blood or trade wars that take away food. For we believe that the weak ones use force, but the strong use dialogue to resolve their conflicts. We also believe that life is God's masterpiece, a spectacle that should never be interrupted by human violence."

The parents rejoiced with these words. Yet the representative of the judges almost fell from the tower. The audience was completely quiet. The world was in awe. People had no idea that the modest educators who lived in the confines of classrooms could carry so much wisdom. The teachers' speech shocked the leaders of the event.

Seeing that the competition's success was in jeopardy, the event mediator brashly declared, "You dreamers! You live outside of reality!". Then, a bold teacher exclaimed in a sensible way: "If we stop dreaming, we will die!". The event organizer felt challenged, so he took the microphone and tried harder to harm the teachers: "Who cares about teachers nowadays? Compare yourselves to the other professions. You do not participate in the most important political meetings. You are rarely mentioned by the press. Society cares little about schools. Look at the salary you receive at the end of the month!". A teacher looked at him and responded confidently, "We do not work just for the salary, but for the love of your children and all the young people in the world."

Furious, the event leader shouted, "Your profession will be extinct in modern societies. Computers will replace you! You are unworthy to be in this competition." This argument manipulated the audience, making them change sides. They condemned the teachers. They praised virtual education. They chanted in unison: "Computers! Computers! The end of teachers!". The stadium went into a frenzy repeating this phrase. They annihilated the teachers. Teachers had never been so humiliated. Blown away by these words, they decided to leave the tower. Do you know what happened?

The tower collapsed. Nobody realized, but the parents and teachers were the ones supporting the tower. It was a shocking scene. The speakers were hospitalized. Subsequently, the teachers took an unimaginable action: they abandoned the classroom for the first time. One attempted to replace them with computers, providing every student with a device. They employed the most cutting-edge multimedia strategies. Now, guess what happened…

Society collapsed. Injustices and miseries of the soul increased even more. Pain and tears expanded. The prison of depression, fear, and anxiety overwhelmed a large part of the population. Violence and crimes multiplied. Human interaction, which was already difficult, became intolerable. Humanity groaned in pain – it was at risk of not surviving. Everyone was shocked to realize that computers could not impart wisdom, solidarity, and love for life. The public had never believed that teachers were the cornerstones of our professions and sustaining our lucidity and intelligence. They found out that the tiny glimmer of hope permeating society came from the hearts of parents and teachers who devoted their lives to educating their children.

Everyone understood that society was living a long and foggy night. Science, politics, and money could not overcome it. They realized that the hope for a beautiful dawn rested on each father, each mother, and each teacher, not on psychiatrists, the judges, the military, or the press. It does not matter if parents live in a palace or a shack, and if teachers teach in a luxurious or a poor school – they are the hope of the world.

In response, in every city across every country, politicians, representatives of professional classes, and businesses held meetings with teachers. They acknowledged that they had committed a crime against education. They apologized and begged them not to abandon their children. Then, they made a decisive promise: They determined that half of the budget they spent on weapons, police apparatus, and the industry of tranquilizers and antidepressants would be invested in education. They promised to restore the dignity of teachers and provide means for every child on Earth to be nourished with food in their bodies and knowledge in their souls. None of them would be without a school anymore. The teachers cried. They were moved by such a promise. For centuries, they had been waiting for society to wake up and notice the drama of education. Regretfully, social miseries had to get out of control before society became aware of them.

However, because they had always been unnamed heroes who cared deeply about every child, adolescent, and young person, the teachers made the decision to go back to the classroom and help every student learn how to navigate the waters of the emotion. For the first time, society had put education at the center of its attention. The sun began to shine after the long storm... The effects showed up after ten years, and twenty years later, everyone was in a state of amazement. Young people no longer gave up on life. There were no more suicides. The use of drugs dissipated. Almost no one heard about mental disorders or violence. And what about prejudice? What even was that? No one remembered its meaning. White people affectionately embraced black ones. Jewish children would sleep at the houses of Palestinian children. Fear vanished, terrorism disappeared, love triumphed.

Prisons became museums. Policemen became poets. Psychiatry offices were empty. Psychiatrists became writers. Judges became musicians. Prosecutors became philosophers. And what about the generals? They discovered the sweet scent of the flowers, they learned to get their hands dirty in order to cultivate them.

What about the world's newspapers and TVs? What did they report, what did they sell? They stopped selling human miseries and tears. They sold dreams, advertised hope...

When will this story become a reality? If we all dream this dream, one day it will come true.

Final Considerations

As I wrote the conclusion of this book, I had the desire to gather some of the teachers from my past, host a dinner for them, and express my gratitude. I also felt compelled to spend time with my parents, not only on holidays, and tell them how much they meant to me. If you harbor a similar wish, do the same. If we don't value our roots, we have no way to endure life's hardships.

The poetic dream of rescuing the value of education, pictured by the story of the great tower, is still a mirage in the social wilderness. While society has not yet awakened, I would like to finish this book by paying tribute to parents and teachers. My limitations are the only reason this tribute is not more eloquent.

A Tribute to The Teachers

We would like to express our gratitude to you on behalf of all students around the world for your unwavering love and support of education up until this day. Many of you have spent the best years of your lives, and some even fell ill during this arduous task.

The social system does not value you in proportion to your greatness, but rest assured that without you, society has no horizon, our nights have no stars, our souls have no health, and our emotions have no joy.

We appreciate your love, wisdom, tears, creativity, insight, both inside and outside the classroom. The world may not applaud you, but the unequivocal knowledge of science must recognize that you are the most important workers to society. Teachers, thank you very much. You are masters of life.

A Tribute to The Parents

On behalf of all children around the world, I thank all you parents for everything you have done for us. Thank you for your advice, affection, scolding, and kisses. Love led you to take all the risks in the world for our sake. You didn't give every child all the things they wanted, but you gave them everything you had.

You gave up on your dreams so we could dream. You sacrificed your leisure so we could have joy. You endured sleepless nights so we could sleep soundly. You shed tears so we could be happy. Forgive us for our mistakes, particularly for failing to recognize how much you are worth. Teach us how to be your friends.

Our debt is immeasurable. We owe you love…

Dear teachers and parents, remember that although time may separate us, people never truly pass away when they are within someone's heart. We will always carry a piece of you within ourselves throughout our story.

The End.

Bibliographic References

ADORNO, T. Educação e Emancipação. Rio de Janeiro: Paz e Terra, 1971.

CURY, Augusto. Inteligência Multifocal, São Paulo: Cultrix, 1998.

_____. Revolucione Sua Qualidade de Vida. Rio de Janeiro: Sextante, 2002.

_____. Análise da Inteligência de Cristo. São Paulo: Academia de Inteligência, 2000.

DURANT, Will. História da Filosofia. Rio de Janeiro: Nova Fronteira, 1996.

GARDNER, Howard. Inteligências Múltiplas. Porto Alegre: Artes Médicas, 1995.

GOLEMAN, Daniel. Inteligência Emocional. Rio de Janeiro: Objetiva, 1996.

FOUCAULT, Michel. "A doença e a existência" in Doença mental e psicologia. Rio de Janeiro: Folha Carioca, 1998.

FREIRE, Paulo. Pedagogia da Autonomia: saberes necessários à prática educativa. Rio de Janeiro: Paz e Terra, 7a edição, 1998.

FREUD, Sigmund. Obras completas de Sigmund Freud. Rio de Janeiro: Imago, 1969.

NIETZSCHE, F. Humano Demasiado Humano. Lisboa: Relógio D'Água, 1997.

PIAGET, Jean. Biologia e conhecimento. Petrópolis: Vozes, 2a edição, 1996.

PLATÃO. "República. Livro VII", in Obras completas, edição bilíngue. Paris: Les Belles Lettres, 1985.

RICOEUR, P. L'homme falible. Paris: Seuil, 1960. SARTRE, Jean-Paul. O ser e o nada. Petrópolis: Vozes, 1997.

VYGOTSKY, L. A formação social da mente. São Paulo: Martins Fontes, 1987.

Here you can read an excerpt from another title by the author:

Digital Intoxication: How to Face the Evil of the Millennium

(Chapter 5) The Mind Lies: Digital Intoxication Has Become a Syndrome

One of the fundamental theses of the Emotion Management program is the acknowledgment that the mind lies. Throughout your life, you may encounter many enemies but no one can be as relentless as your own mind if you fail to manage your thoughts and emotions. The mind will lie, causing you to suffer in advance, to anguish over future problems. Parents often hold their babies and worry they will become drug addicts or might suffer accidents or even be victims of diseases.

Your mind will lie to you, making up fears related to your work, finances, or even the government of your country, convincing you of your inability to overcome these challenges. The mind will lie, telling you to dwell on your past, to brood over grievances, frustrations, and dislikes. The mind sells worries, charging a high price: a "Self" who fails to manage its mind may fall victim to countless anxieties, expend more energy than it can replenish during sleep, and wake up literally exhausted. The mind "lies" that life lacks meaning, that everything is boring, that there is no reason to live, although there are millions of reasons for that, and the biggest one is simply being alive.

From a distance, in a superficial analysis, you may find many spectacular people, apparently coherent, measured, patient and altruistic. However, upon closer examination, no one is fully free and healthy. The more a human being irresponsibly consumes emotional lies of their mind the greater their susceptibility to illness. They may deceive those around them; however, they cannot deceive themselves. They may sell an image of a hero, but inside there is a fragile human being who needs to be embraced.

The more accelerated and agitated the human mind is in the era of digital intoxication, the more it will lie to this human being, trapping the Self. The mind brings the idea that beauty is cruelly comparative, while, in reality, beauty is in the eyes of the beholder, so it cannot be bought or compared. Yet, thousands of people post on social media a toned, well-shaped, impeccable body, resembling Barbie dolls, unaware this standard enters the collective unconscious mind and destroys the self-esteem of millions of people, especially girls, generating an illness I call the Unattainable Beauty Standard (UBS) syndrome or Barbie syndrome, with prominent symptoms such as self-punishment, self-criticism, fragmented self-image, low self-esteem, continuous feeling of comparison, rejection of one or more areas of the body, discomfort in front of mirrors, and need to dress for the eyes of others. That's why I wrote the book "The Beauty Dictatorship and the Women's Revolution."

Parents and teachers should lead their children and students since childhood to rebel against the dictatorial beauty standard. I always gave dolls to my three daughters, Camila, Carol, and Claudia, who were chubby and dark-skinned. I wanted them to deeply understand that every human being, regardless of skin color, was unique and irreplaceable. I also wanted to train them to internalize that every human being, regardless of body type, was beautiful and irreplaceable. They learned how to be leaders of themselves, despite all the antics and conflicts that children have, especially the two youngest ones.

Two of my daughters had fuller figures in adolescence, but I emphasized that they were beautiful, that what was wrong was the beauty standard imposed by the media. I explained that the beauty dictatorship aimed to generate anxiety, to boost consumption, because a person who is unhappy with their body consumes more. And I said that many photographic models were also victims. Statistics have shown that they suffer 20% more than other women. Using tools for emotional management, my daughters learned how to deal well with social stigma, they reignited their self-image, raised their self-esteem, and took charge of their story.

The journey with my daughters has been wonderful. I love being with them. One of my biggest criticisms is not with people, but with time. Time is cruel, since between childhood and old age it only takes a few moments. It is regrettable that life is so brief. In this tiny existence, our goal, as parents and children, must be to expand time so that we can live unforgettable moments in unique times. I sought to expand emotional time not only by criticizing unhealthy beauty standards or teaching emotional management tools, but also making the most from the limited time we had. For example: although I was very busy, I led Camila, Carol, and Claudia to discover the nuances of flowers and the details that were imperceptible to the eyes of the hurried and anxious ones. In this digital age, parents must be very concerned with socioemotional education, in order to neutralize artificial life on social media.

At night, while traveling along the roads, I urged them to look at a point of light on the farms and nurtured their empathy, as well as their capacity to fall in love with life, and to contemplate beauty. I would inquire: who are the inhabitants of that house? What tears have they shed? What dreams do they have? What nightmares haunt them? What adventures do they live? Perhaps they may not remember many of the experiences we shared; however, they are there, in their unconscious minds; shaping their personalities through affective memories. I have often spoken to them about my challenges and frustrations because I did not want them to orbit around a famous person or a psychiatrist who was above emotional illnesses, but rather a simple human being under construction, who bought commas to write their story, even when the world was crumbling around them.

They learned how to journey within themselves and to realize that life, despite all its pains and difficulties, was a unique and unmissable spectacle. Therefore, they became my best friends, each other's best friends, and collectors of friends.

Expand time, since between childhood and old age there are only a few moments. Those around you are more important than millions of views, social recognition, applause in stadiums, or having your name on the list of the wealthiest.

DIGITAL INTOXICATION IS A SYNDROME

One of the most serious consequences of the excessive usage of digital devices is tampering with the black box of thought and emotion construction, altering the entire functioning of the mind. That results in digital intoxication, characterized as an emotional syndrome. Digital devices interfere with dopamine and serotonin cycle, which are two brain neurotransmitters. Let me make a quick comment about them.

Serotonin affects mood, appetite, sleep, and sexual desire. And because it influences emotional states, it ends up interfering with memory, both in recording and accessing it. Dopamine also affects emotional states, the reward center in response to achievements and frustrations, memory, muscle activity, among others. They are erroneously called "happiness molecules." Although these neurotransmitters affect mood, when acting alone they do not produce stable, deep pleasure, imbued with empathy, self-control, and contemplation of beauty. Cocaine, amphetamines, and other drugs can alter the cycle of these neurotransmitters, which causes dangerous fluctuations, increasing and decreasing their levels rapidly. All of this leads to dependency.

Anything that acts rapidly on the center of emotions, whether by exciting or calming it, thereby generating expansions and deficits in response, can easily produce psychological dependence. Slow-acting antidepressants rarely cause dependence – for example, selective serotonin reuptake inhibitors like fluoxetine, paroxetine. But fast-acting tranquilizers, like lorazepam, have a high risk of causing dependence if not used carefully regarding its dosage and duration. Cocaine and crack overstimulate the dopamine and serotonin cycle, leading to a rebound depression. What is the result of that? The AMR phenomenon records double P killer windows, which are feedback loops, forming mental prisons, and causing the user to need increasingly higher doses, as psychoadaptation decreases the pleasure experience, generating high psychological dependence.

Similarly to stimulant drugs, social networks stimulate the serotonin and dopamine cycle, which generates a high level of excitability with the quantity of likes, views, social evidence, or even with the atrocious alternation of images, and then frustration is generated because it is an artificial world. What is the result of that? High psychological dependence, akin to cocaine. And just like it, millions of users have anxious needs to spend more and more time on digital devices, to feel less and less pleasure.

I have given various training sessions for judges, including for the Federal Police, and have warned these noble professionals about the risks posed to the emotional health of the world's youth. We are in the era of mental prisons and emotional beggars. But unfortunately, the indiscriminate use of social networks and video games is a socially accepted and commercially free drug. There should be limits for children. I will talk about that. However, in early childhood, a child should just be a child, and should be away from the digital world. Tampering with the dopamine and serotonin cycle is extremely serious, representing an unimaginable threat to their emotional and intellectual future.

The digital world has brought increased productivity for companies, expanded sociability and increased access to information. Something worthy of applause. But the excessive use of digital devices, social networks and video games creates chaos in the human psyche. When Steve Jobs launched his first smartphone in 2007, he had no idea about the psychological dependence, emotional disorders, and countless suicides these devices would indirectly cause. But they caused it all! Silicon Valley has a gigantic debt to the world's youth. Research needs to be conducted to prove what is glaringly obvious to many psychiatrists, psychologists, teachers, and parents.

> *Freedom is fundamental, but indiscriminately giving digital devices to children during meal times, playtime, study time, and times for dialogue and interaction is an alarming crime.*

If you have any doubt about whether digital devices interfere with the dopamine and serotonin cycles, causing emotional dependence, take away a cellphone from a teenager who uses it for more than two or three hours a day and observe the withdrawal symptoms appear. Digital intoxication syndrome is an illness with several symptoms:

- Fatigue upon waking up – Sleep becomes non-restorative.
- Irritability – Minor stressful stimuli disturb greatly.
- Anxiety.
- Intolerance to frustrations – Difficulty in dealing with losses, disappointments, haters, criticisms.
- Sad mood tending towards depression – Sadness builds, but depressive mood destroys.
- Mental exhaustion accompanied by psychosomatic symptoms.
- Insomnia or poor-quality sleep.
- Sense of existential emptiness – Lack of meaning and purpose in life.
- Neurotic need for social validation.
- Neurotic need for comparison.
- Disgust towards boredom – Rejection of daily routine, feeling that one is not doing anything important if not connected. Nothing common motivates or enchants.
- Aversion to solitude – Aversion to being alone, to introspection, to seeking oneself.

The first seven symptoms are common to a variety of anxiety crises, such as Generalized Anxiety Disorder (GAD), Obsessive-Compulsive Disorder

(OCD), burnout syndrome and even accelerated thinking syndrome. But the last five are characteristics of the digital intoxication syndrome. It is worth noting that millions of children are not getting proper sleep, often without their parents noticing, because the blue wavelength emitted by digital device screens reduces melatonin levels, a molecule that triggers and stabilizes sleep. This is extremely serious. You may have debtors throughout your life who will demand payment, but nobody will charge the bill as much as insomnia or poor-quality sleep.

The triggering and intensifying source of many mental illnesses is called insomnia. Everything gets worse with it, including psychosomatic illnesses. Those who do not sleep need to engage in physical exercise to release endorphins, they need to train emotion management techniques, they need to slow down their minds and overcome their conflicts. And if they still cannot sleep even after doing all of this, they should see a doctor, preferably a psychiatrist. Mild insomnia can greatly improve with psychotherapy, with the intervention of a psychologist. But be warned, stubborn insomnia, lasting for days or weeks, is very dangerous. Most anxiety crises, severe depressive crises, or suicide attempts are preceded by cumulative insomnia.

Minds saturated with information cause agitated emotions

A ten-year-old boy today has more information, due to continuous internet connection, than John Kennedy did when he was president of the USA, at the height of the Cold War. The result is not only Accelerated Thinking Syndrome (ATS), characterized by the first seven symptoms mentioned above, along with hyperthinking, concentration deficit, difficulty in dealing with slow-paced individuals, and memory deficit, but also digital intoxication syndrome, which, as I have said, touches on the central point of aversion to boredom and loneliness, the lack of meaning in life, and the anxious needs to be the center of social attention and to compare oneself with peers. It is no wonder that many highly successful digital influencers end up emotionally collapsing. They altered the dopamine and serotonin cycles.

A particular and serious message to influencers. You may be an influencer on various social networks, but you should know that digital intoxication is lurking to trap you. Protecting your emotional well-being greatly helps if you do not live for likes, numbers of interactions or outsource your mental health to criticisms and haters. It may be helpful to know that you are a mere mortal and your main function is not to have the maximum number of views, but to contribute to humanity. Be alert.

Those who live "in" and "from" the digital world should know that the problem is not whether you will get ill or intoxicated, but when you will get ill and to what extent will you become intoxicated. Taking strategic breaks is crucial. Have one or two sabbatical months annually. Or a whole year off every five years. "But I'll lose millions of followers!" So what? Test if your content has social relevance. And if you lose, at least you will not lose yourself. What is the point of being the most notable influencer in a graveyard? Many of those who applaud or like you today will forget you in a week.

The poor artificial intelligence compared to the sophisticated human mind

Thinking is not just an option for *Homo sapiens*, but also an inevitability. If the Self, which is the leader of the human mind, the agent of autonomy and choice does not consciously read memory and produce thoughts in a logical direction, four co-pilots of the Self (Memory Trigger, Windows, Emotional Anchor, and Autoflow) will read the memory, producing thoughts and emotions without its conscious mind authorization. Have you ever been impressed that your mind is a continuous factory of thoughts? We think things that leave us perplexed, making us wonder, "how did this arise in my mind?". You do not think just because you want to, but because there is a surprising constructive flow of unconscious phenomena in your mind and mine.

Some people tell me, upon seeing my explanation about the psyche: "Dr. Cury, I did not realize I was so complicated and complex like this." I reply: "Neither did I." We are all very complex intellectually and sophisticatedly complicated. Each thought is built and deconstructed in a continuous and inevitable process. Similarly, albeit at a slower pace, emotion is in a continuous constructive state. Therefore, one common and great misconception in psychology, which we sometimes reproduce, is that a person must be "balanced". The mind is never balanced, otherwise, it would interrupt its flow. I reiterate, our psyche lives in an inevitable process of construction, deconstruction, and reconstruction. To deconstruct, there must be imbalance. What is not healthy is being an excessively uncontrolled, hyper-reactive, unstable person. For example, someone who is calm in the morning, irritable at lunch, intolerable in the afternoon, and unable to tolerate themselves at night.

As the Self is shaped, the child begins to interact and building bridges by using two major types of conscious thoughts: the dialectical thinking, which copies language symbols, being the most logical and operational; and the antidialectical, which is imaginative thinking, challenging the control of the Self, and not following the matrices of phonetic language or signs. Now, I have a question for you: before entering school, does a child ask a lot or a little? We know they ask a lot! Why? Because curiosity, exploratory capacity, and the search for pleasure, do not depend on the Self, but on the flow of thought construction.

Yet, what kind of thinking does the child use to foster questions and explore their potential? Dialectical or anti-dialectical thinking? Anti-dialectical. Before entering school, children ask a lot because they unleash their imagination, but over time, school stifles antidialectical thinking, and the disastrous consequence is fewer and fewer questions asked. Thus, they imprison questioners and kill thinkers.

At university, most students remain silent when there should be a great debate of ideas. For example: at USP (University of São Paulo State), where I teach in master's and doctoral programs, I need to tease my students. They are fascinating young people, but they have lost their audacity because of the conventional educational system, which uses atrocious and insane pedagogy to educate. Educating is not teaching the answer but ignite questions. Schools remove the oxygen from the art of asking questions with their Cartesian system, and in this century, the digital world has emerged, which buried the art of questioning. Young people and adults, with due exceptions, became passive consumers of the digital world, rarely questioning what they see or hear.

Another question: is suffering about the future a complex thought? Yes, it is, because you anticipate a nonexistent future in your imagination. Do you think a robot equipped with Artificial Intelligence (AI), no matter how advanced, will suffer about the future or develop feelings of guilt any day? Never! Everyone is fascinated by artificial intelligence, but no AI or robot will feel loneliness or anxiety, nor will it experience self-punishment or self-blame, much less think about the purpose of life or have suicidal thoughts. These are attributes of the "anti-dialectical anti-language" mental system merged with emotionality.

Even if ChatGPT has a thousand generations and achieves singularity, passing the Turing test a thousand times (in which you cannot say if it is a human or a robot), the AI will only have dialectical thinking as its language, albeit incredibly fast, sophisticated, and with a much better capacity for organizing data and providing responses than ours. AI does not have and will never have imaginative thinking, a result of anti-language; much less the emotional capacity to experience the indescribable spectacle of love or produce the simplest feeling of nostalgia.

Anti-dialectical thoughts have a greater power to drag our emotions than the power of dialectical thoughts. You think dialectically "I want to be calm," yet achieving tranquility is not easy, but imagining "tomorrow I will have a problem to solve," tension levels increase, and it may even give you butterflies in your stomach. Therefore, motivation techniques rarely work, also, the emotional hell is full of well-intentioned people who have not learned how to minimally manage their minds. I have much to say on this topic, but it will be done in the book "The End of Emotional Intelligence and the Beginning of Emotional Management."

Now, a dire warning for you: remember that thinking is not just an option of the Self, but an inevitable process, as the unconscious phenomena, which are supporting actors of the Self, are highly active and will produce thoughts. For example, as you read this book, the mental trigger is being activated in waves (first phenomenon), opening thousands of windows (second), the emotional anchor gets pinned and causing focus and concentration (third), and the self-flow (fourth) is reading and rereading the open windows within the anchor's focus. When reading books, driving vehicles, or experiencing spontaneous internalizations, the Self is often less active. Have you ever walked for miles on a road and suddenly your Self awakens and asks how did I get here? It happened through the copilots.

When the windows opened by the mental trigger, whether through an intrapsychic stimulus (for example, a disturbing thought) or social (an offense), are traumatic, this will generate hyperfocus; consequently, it will produce phobic, disproportionate, or aggressive reactions. The Self must come into action and give a shock of lucidity to open the window and recycle stressful emotions and thoughts. But rarely does anyone do mental hygiene. In this case, the brain's biographer, relentlessly, will archive and pollute the cerebral cortex. Sometimes I am stressed, but I do not know why. I am depressed, but I have no reason. My heart is racing and I am short of breath, but I do not understand why, so I think it is because of the vaccine I took. In times of Covid-19 vaccine has become an excuse for everything, regardless of side effects being discovered. The individual does not take a mental shower per month or per year, does not take an emotional shower throughout their life, how can they not have an anxious, contaminated mind.

> *The Self drives and constructs dialectical, linguistic, and logical thought more easily. However, it has more difficulty managing antidialectical or imaginary thought. This is a central paradox, a fundamental conflict, of Homo sapiens.*

You can build thousands of thoughts on academic theses, work goals, economy, sports, politics, as they are dialectical thoughts, easily manipulable, however preventing suffering from anticipation or a worry that assaults your tranquility is not as simple, because they are antidialectical, difficult to dissipate.

You manage machines, companies, cities, states, but you will need training and humility to drive the mental vehicle. It is no wonder that many doctors, lawyers, executives, educators, are masters at work, but live in hell at home, filled with friction, arguments over trivial matters, endless criticism, altered tone of voice, tears. They have a neurotic need to change the other.

However, despite all the limitations of the Self to manage antidialectical or imaginary thought in hyperfocus, if it does not give a shock of lucidity to its production and liberate it to produce dreams, life projects, empathy, healthy relationships, it will be dominated by mental ghosts (including self-punishment, fear of the future, blackmail, harsh sentencing of loved ones, aversion to boredom and loneliness: "There's nothing to do in this house").

We all accumulate mental garbage and produce "madness" in our minds, but having a passive spectator Self that does not question everything, that does not challenge our conformity and victim mentality, that does not confront our criticism, that does not recycle our uncontrollable ability to point out flaws and withhold praise, is to be a cruel enemy of your emotional health, your family, and your business.

Always remember that...

...A special message to the youth and especially to influencers. You may be an influencer on various social media platforms, but be aware that digital intoxication is lurking to trap you. It greatly helps your emotional protection if you do not live for likes, numbers of interactions, or outsource your mental health to criticisms and haters. It may also help you understand that you are just a mortal and your primary function is not to have the maximum number of views, but to contribute to humanity.

However, be alert: those who live "in" and "of" the digital world should know that the problem is not "whether" you will get ill or intoxicated, but "when" you will get ill and "to what extent" you will get intoxicated. It would be very important to take strategic breaks. Have one or two sabbatical months annually. Or a whole year off every five years. "But I will lose millions of followers!" So what? Test if your content has social relevance, if it contributes to humanity. And if you lose, at least you will not lose yourself. What's the point of being the most notable influencer in a graveyard? Many of those who applaud or like you today will forget you in a week. Do not abandon yourself, look out for yourself.

Review Request

Before you go, can I ask you for a quick favor?

Would you please leave this book an honest review on Amazon?

Your review won't take long, but it can help this book reach more readers like you.

Thank you for reading, and thank you so much for being part of the journey.

-Augusto

www.ingramcontent.com/pod-product-compliance
Lightning Source LLC
Chambersburg PA
CBHW022108090426
42743CB00008B/766